LOVED ON PURPOSE

LOVED ON PURPOSE

STACY SORRELL

Xulon Press

Xulon Press
2301 Lucien Way #415
Maitland, FL 32751
407.339.4217
www.xulonpress.com

© 2019 by Stacy Sorrell

All rights reserved solely by the author. The author guarantees all contents are original and do not infringe upon the legal rights of any other person or work. No part of this book may be reproduced in any form without the permission of the author. The views expressed in this book are not necessarily those of the publisher.

Unless otherwise indicated, Scripture quotations taken from the Christian Standard Bible. (CSB). Copyright © 2017 by Holman Bible Publishers. Used by permission. All rights reserved.

Scripture quotations taken from the Holy Bible, New International Version (NIV). Copyright © 1973, 1978, 1984, 2011 by Biblica, Inc.™. Used by permission. All rights reserved.

Scripture quotations taken from the King James Version (KJV)–*public domain.*

Printed in the United States of America.

ISBN-13: 978-1-5456-7596-0

DEDICATION

I WANT TO GIVE GOD ALL THE GLORY FOR THE completion of this book and how far he has brought me. I didn't know I had the gift of writing, but I knew I had a story—a story that I was once ashamed to share—but after God delivered me, I realized it was His victory over my circumstances that I was sharing. Frankly, I'm only boasting of God's greatness and faithfulness, that He would help me frame my story to share, overflowing with a burning hope that others, like me, would be made whole and free. May each of my readers experience the unfailing, matchless love of our heavenly Father!

> *Love is patient, love is kind. It does not envy, it does not boast, it is not proud. It does not dishonor others, it is not self-seeking, it is not easily angered, it keeps no record of wrongs. Love does not delight in evil but rejoices with the truth. It always protects, always trusts, always hopes, always perseveres. Love never fails.*
>
> *– 1 Corinthians 13:4-8*

I want to thank my family and friends for their patience and loving support while I embarked on this new journey. A very special thank you goes out to my children, Jordan, Haniyyah and KJ; they have been my biggest support and have encouraged me every step of the way. Mommy loves you all very much!

Thank you, Haniyyah, for your breathtaking artwork and vision for the book cover. It blesses me so much.

Table of Contents

Dedication vii
Foreword xi

1 – THE SEARCH BEGINS 1
2 – STILL UNFULFILLED 11
3 – SHATTERED AND BROKEN 23
4 – LOST AND REMOVED 35
5 – MISPLACED AND DAZED 45
6 – THE SEARCH CONTINUES 53
7 – TRUE LOVE REVEALED ITSELF 61
8 – MY PURPOSE 75

Author's Note 85

Foreword

---∝---

"And we know that God works all things together for good to those who love God, to those who are called according to His purpose."

– Romans 8:28

MY PRECIOUS READERS, THIS MOST BELOVED Scripture verse summarizes my story and says it all: every moment of despair, all your deep heartache and flowing tears, every disappointment, every loss, God is working together for His good, weaving it into a tapestry of Love for you. Though you may not see it now and cannot feel it, He is right now knitting all your sorrow into a vibrant picture of peace and joy that only He can give—as you trust Him with your present, with your past, and with your future.

My heart is overflowing with gratitude to Him ... and with expectation as well, for you to delve into these pages and discover it for yourself: the important, beautiful Truth that—no matter how much your heart is breaking, no matter the shame you feel or the angst of this world—you can turn to Him, cry out to Him, put your faith in Him, and trust Him with your life. God is using it all as you, too, discover that you are Loved on Purpose. And let me tell you, there's nothing better in this life as you prepare your heart for the best Love of all.

Join me on this perilous, magnificent, victorious journey, won't you?

1 – THE SEARCH BEGINS

―――∝―――

WITHOUT WARNING, HE SHOWS UP AT MY front door after school one day, standing nonchalantly with his hands in his pockets and a smirk on his face. Scurrying to answer his repeated knocks, I swing the door open and blink back the light now cascading past me.

"Oh, I know you," I think to myself, "just the guy at school always cracking jokes."

"Jason around?" he asks peering inside, his eyes darting through the living room and into the kitchen.

"My brother? Nope, not home."

Thinking he'll just turn and leave, I'm not too talkative, my mind still focused on the next day's seventh grade history test.

He shifts his feet and looks me up and down. "Hey, can I use your bathroom?"

"Uh, sure, I guess so ... no problem." *I wince, my mom's words echoing in my head. I know I'm not supposed to have house guests while my parents are at work, but he seems harmless enough. He'll just be here a few moments anyway.*

Yet, without question, this marks a turning point in my young life: a moment I will forever regret.

He starts off cracking jokes, lingering too long as I try to politely direct him out the door. Suddenly his hand darts out, quickly grabbing my wrist, and my heart drops to my stomach. Terrified and panicked beyond anything I've ever known, I see him turn into a raging animal, no longer the class clown I recognize. Strong and angry with eyes full of hate, he attacks me.

My innocence ... is literally ripped from my body by this classmate. And I am never the same.

Friends, as I write this memory, my fingers hesitating over the keyboard, I can still picture the horror of this scene and remember the physical pain. I can still find myself back there, sobbing ... trembling ... traumatized. I never thought the sexual assault of anal rape at the age of 12 would so drastically and negatively impact my preteen and teenage years and leave its fingerprints upon my soul.

After he finally flees the house, I clean myself up and tell no one, not even my closest friends. Returning back to junior high the next day, I'm full of fear, embarrassment, and shame. I can't wait to graduate eighth grade the following year and begin high school on the other side of town—so I'll never have to see his face or his friends' faces walking the hallways again.

When I fast-forward several decades, I can see how this experience would haunt me years after. But at the time, I was simply trying to make it through each day, immersed in an intense daily struggle. As the first days of high school began, I quickly realized how badly I hated it. The girls intimidated me, and the boys scared me. I always tried to fit in with the popular girls, but just when I thought I was gaining ground, I always got rejected. My insecurities made me a bit paranoid, and I began to wonder if they all knew my secret, what happened to me on that day in seventh grade. Stuck in my brokenness, I imagined them believing his lies over my truths. I felt them judging me, no one understanding my pain or who I really was.

And then my search was on—my pursuit of acceptance, my desire to be liked at any cost. No one knew my deep, horrible secret, however, and at times I blamed myself. Most of all, I didn't want my parents ever finding out about this horrific assault. I didn't want them feeling the agony of my torment; that's how much I loved them. I couldn't bear to see the pain of *my pain* in their eyes. Often hiding my anguish with laughter and humor, I attempted to forget my past and wipe from my memory every last remnant of this despicable trauma—and move forward.

My toxic quest of self-discovery, companionship, and acceptance was set to begin. Immersed in the thick of peer pressure and insecurity, my mind still reeling in days of deep angst, I mentally struggled with if I was even still a virgin after being victimized by rape. I really liked boys but was deathly afraid to have sex. Sometimes I flirted and giggled with them but had no desire for a serious boyfriend.

At 16, I finally did lose my virginity ... although I was filled with anxiety during this intimate moment as haunting memories of my first sexual encounter flooded my mind. I was curious about what sex with someone you love was like, but mostly I wanted to please my boyfriend, whom I absolutely adored; I didn't want to risk losing him, so I finally gave in and gave away the most valuable part of me.

Throughout this time before I graduated high school, I began to see the value of cherishing my body, realizing I deserved to be treated with love and respect, but this was my very first boyfriend-girlfriend relationship. He attended another high school, soon relocated to college, and our three-year relationship was over.

Was I hurt by this break-up? That's an understatement. My naive mind had thoughts of us getting married and living happily ever after. At such a young age, I was then back on the prowl in the dating scene, hoping to find the man of my dreams.

Now looking back, I can see how most high school graduates are clueless in choosing their career path, but I was completely lost. I had no professional desires. As high school was so emotionally unbearable, I scarcely showed up for classes, and as you can imagine, this left my grades in dire need of emergency resuscitation. So, while I decided to attend junior college, I attended only to please my parents. My laser-like focus: to get married and have children. Raised by both parents with two sisters and a brother, I always desired to have the same family dynamics as my parents enjoyed. One thing was for sure—my father always prayed with all of us, and we attended church as a family quite often. As a child, I didn't realize the critical importance of a spiritual upbringing and how a spiritual foundation would later save my life. As close and loving as my family was, I still felt a strong sadness within me. Maybe, I thought, true love would disperse the darkness I was feeling. Sometimes when I reflect on my past, I'm right back there, a girl with lots of budding dreams, and I can feel those same emotions.

As a girl in junior college, getting dates is easy—that's never hard for me. I can gain a man's attention, but when I look in the mirror, I don't see beauty. It's an indescribable mindset, for sure. The more attention I gain from men, the more I'm filled with the temporary satisfaction and confidence I crave—and then the more my desire for that feeling continues to escalate. As I try to focus on a career path, one deeply-held desire keeps emerging: my dream of becoming a model. When I open up and share that dream with friends and family, though, they laugh and change the topic or say things like, "Girl, you can't be a model," or, "You're too old to start a modeling career." But that doesn't stop my efforts.

The new guy I've been dating is extremely religious and practices celibacy. He's looking for a wife, and I'm looking for a husband. So needless to say, we've connected quickly. We often read the Bible together, so I've decided to try celibacy with him.

Though we've only dated a short while, I continue to read my Bible and be celibate, too. I even got off birth control, set on a new path. I work multiple jobs, take classes at the community college, and revel in my new, straight-arrow life; it's depicting the new me I'm destined to be, and I'm going to prove all my haters wrong. I've started to love myself again and look forward to a future, something I've never felt before.

But then I see him; and the memory, so painful, snaps me back to reality.

I was walking in the mall with my friend Peyton, and as he walked by me, I was mesmerized. About to exit the mall doors, I did something I'd never done before: I turned around to see where he went. As I turned the corner, he turned around as well, and we bumped right into one another. We both laughed, and he said, "How you doin', beautiful?" And my heart stopped! I was instantly in awe of him as he introduced himself as Josh. I replied with a flirtatious giggle, we quickly exchanged phone numbers, and at that moment, my life began a different path.

In fact, that moment in time was incredible for me—like eternity standing still. His voice on the phone was so endearing, and I was so excited for our first date. He picked me up from work, and I was so shy. As he was much older than me, he also quickly intimidated me, plus he was so very handsome and charming. Over dinner

I blushed the entire time, but he was such a gentleman, opening every restaurant and car door. I immediately began thinking that an older man was exactly what I needed. *No more will I date immature boys after this experience*, I thought. A few more dates followed, and already I was emotionally invested. He made me laugh, and he always told me how beautiful I was. You know, he made me feel so good about myself.

After dating him for a short four weeks, he told me in multiple conversations how he was looking for a committed relationship. He also told me how he and the mother of his two children didn't get along, and that they had broken up months prior to him meeting me. I was relieved he was opening up to me as I was also opening up to him. He finally invited me over to his home, proof he was really into me with no hidden secrets. Clearly, if he invited me to his home, he wasn't seeing anyone else, and after spending more time there with him, I began to feel more and more comfortable. I know I was practicing celibacy, but he was very attractive and very touchy feely. I didn't want to risk him not liking me anymore or replacing me, so I decided to break my plans to restrain from sex 'til marriage and agreed to start an intimate relationship with him.

Just weeks later, his calls to me suddenly became infrequent ... and soon stopped altogether. His behavior contradicted all the early promises he had made. Quickly starting to feel abandoned and completely foolish for my decision, I began to pick up my Bible again and focus on moving forward, regretting ever meeting him. Enwrapped once more in that awful insecure feeling, I turned my eyes to my modeling career and dove into work and school, hoping to forget him.

Thankfully, my friend Peyton was dating Josh's friend, Kenny, who could illuminate what really happened. Kenny informed Peyton that Josh was in jail! — and that's why I wasn't hearing from him. I was extremely concerned for his well-being but ecstatic he hadn't abandoned me. Very confused as to why he was in jail since

1 – The Search Begins

he made an honest living as a barber and contractor, I patiently waited for his call. For the next few days I woke up extremely nauseous, but my mind was set on Josh's welfare, not on what was happening with my body.

Being pregnant was the furthest thing from my mind because we were careful. Peyton persuaded me to take a pregnancy test, and I stood there in complete shock and disbelief of the positive test result. That's when it hit me: my life as I knew it was over. How was I going to tell my parents? For all they knew, I was single and celibate. I was now in a very complicated and confusing place, trying to wrap my mind around such overwhelming news. I was hoping now more than ever to receive a call from Josh so I could share this shocking news with him.

Josh called. After picking up the phone, I hurried outside and sat in my car to talk to him as I couldn't risk my parents or siblings overhearing us. I was so relieved! I couldn't wait to tell him I was pregnant and finally hear his words of loving support. As I had been dealing with this news alone, keeping the heavy secret from my family was becoming unbearable. It felt good to be vulnerable with him, but I couldn't wait any longer; I blurted it out, all in one run-on sentence of pain and turmoil and confusion.

But there was complete silence on the other end of the line, and you could have heard a pin drop.

Then Josh began to laugh, his voice now completely changed. He sounded totally different as he said, "I'm sorry to hear about that, but I can't be having more kids right now. I'm dealing with this jail situation. You need to schedule an appointment for an abortion."

I sat in stunned disbelief. I couldn't believe this sweet, charming man whom I had met three months prior was acting so cold toward me. I told him I didn't think I could get an abortion, and while I was explaining my reasons, he cut me off in mid-sentence, snapping in anger, "You know what? You don't have a choice because I'm married." He continued confessing all the other lies he had told me.

He said if I decided to keep the baby I would end up being a complete loser because he wasn't going to be around to care for the child emotionally or financially. He was intentionally trying to hurt me and break me so he could force me into having an abortion. My heart fell out of my chest; I couldn't even respond, and he hung up. At that moment I knew I would never talk to him again. I ran into the house, full of fear and holding back a torrent of tears. I didn't know whom to turn to or what to do.

Josh's reaction to the pregnancy gave me every reason to abort my unborn child, but for some reason, I couldn't do it. Months prior, I had begun reading the Bible, gaining more biblical knowledge. And so I knew better. I couldn't wrap my heart around killing my unborn child simply because Josh was going to be absent from our lives. My heart was already wanting this child, but my mind would sometimes wander, filled with "what ifs." *What if everyone says I'm crazy? What if my dreams to be a model are now dashed? What if my parents pass out when they find out I'm pregnant by a married man? What if I have to go through this pregnancy alone!?*

After praying and crying out to God, I decided to keep my baby. I planned to continue school and work, and to raise my child as a single mother. Even though I made this spiritual decision, I was scared and deeply saddened by my circumstances. I wasn't married, and the father of this child had vanished. I knew I had to tell my parents soon, but I didn't know how ... I was disappointed in myself. And soon I found depression creeping into my mind and body. It seemed easier to just disappear rather than face all the judgment I would soon be up against.

My friend, Tara, drug me out of the house, trying to cheer me up, and we ended up at the mall. I was only about six weeks pregnant and barely showing. Then, when we ran into my high school crush, Isaac, my face lit up. Seeing him put the biggest smile on face, and for five seconds I forgot about my circumstances. Isaac immediately hugged me and held me tight, lifting me up off the ground. As soon as my feet were planted once more, Isaac gave me a passionate kiss on the lips. My head was swimming, completely shocked by his excitement and boldness. Isaac had sometimes called me throughout my teenage years, but after high school I had always had a boyfriend so we could never date or hang out. I was so delighted to see him after all these years. He was gorgeous and smelled nice, too. Can you tell I was completely captivated and delighted?

He asked me if he could take me out on a date, and while I was very apprehensive as I was pregnant, I said "yes," and we exchanged numbers. When we parted, I turned away, feeling overjoyed by his gentle spirit and also realizing that he and I were standing in the exact same area of the mall where I had met Josh just four months prior. As Tara and I walked back to her car, I finally had something to look forward to; even if we went on just one date, it would be worth it and gave me hope in a very dark place.

I didn't know if I should tell Isaac I was pregnant right away. I didn't want him to reject me, hoping to experience the company of a good friend and forget about my problems just for a moment.

But I didn't have long to wait, to consider the right approach or best timing, because he called the next day. So happy to talk with him, I had thought about him non-stop since that magical moment of our unexpected encounter the night before. After some small talk, catching up on old times, he asked if I were dating anyone.

"No, no one at all," I quickly replied.

"Uh, great ... well, do you have plans tonight?"

"No," I again answered right away.

"Can I pick you up tonight and take you out on a date?"

Then I became silent, nervous and scared. I knew I had to tell him I was pregnant, but I was afraid of his reaction.

Repeating himself again, he asked, "Can I? Can I take you out tonight, Stacy?"

"Oh, Isaac, it's just really bad timing … you really don't want to date me right now."

"Why? Do you have a boyfriend??"

"Oh, no, not at all …"

"Then what would keep me from wanting to date you?"

"Isaac, I'm pregnant."

The silence lasted only a moment before he hesitantly asked, "Are you going to be with the guy?"

"Absolutely not."

"Well, then I'll see you tonight at 7."

Shocked, I said, "Okay, sure." I couldn't believe he was still interested in going out with me, knowing I was pregnant. Who was this guy? Who sent him? I rushed home to prepare for our date, hoping he would show up and didn't change his mind.

My doorbell rang, and it was him standing there; he grabbed my hand, walked me to his car, and opened my door, and as he walked to his side of the car, I sat there thanking God and feeling like a princess. For some strange reason, I instantly knew he was heaven-sent and wasn't going to leave my side like everyone else. After our first few dates and long conversations, I knew he was sent to rescue me from all my troubles. God had answered my prayers and sent me an earthly angel!

———∝———

Do not be anxious about anything, but in every situation, by prayer and petition, with thanksgiving, present your requests to God.

– Philippians 4:6

2 – STILL UNFULFILLED

HE DOESN'T CARE THAT I'M PREGNANT WITH another man's child. He really doesn't care! He's just so happy to be in my company, and … honestly? I feel like it's a dream.

I'm constantly thinking, "How can this be? Is it really possible for someone to really love and accept me as I am—pregnant with another man's child?" Maybe I should slow things down a bit because once my stomach begins to show, he'll definitely leave me—like everyone else has.

No, I'll just take one day at a time. Not get my hopes up. And prepare my heart for disappointment. I'll enjoy each day we share together until he leaves my side. After all, Isaac is a wonderful man, but who would ever stick around to care for another man's child?

Looking back on my thoughts that defined that precarious time, I'm still in awe of Isaac's heart, his gracious spirit and obvious love and care for me—all so undeserved. Who knew that God would protect and provide for me so well? Definitely not this girl back then. And through it all, I just kept wondering, "Will it really last?"

Despite my worries, the inevitable happened. No, he didn't leave me; instead, after just a few dates and long conversations, I found myself falling for him. And after he met my family just a few times, they were all enraptured as well. You know, he made us all laugh. He brought a warming peace; he was such a joy to be around. Time was passing so quickly, and I was approaching my fourth month of pregnancy. But I still hadn't told my parents I was pregnant! I know, I know. I knew it must be done, but how?

Isaac and I had an intense talk about this, and I treasured his advice. He was my best friend, the only one who truly understood everything about me. He'd seen my high anxiety at the thought of telling my parents. When they discovered who *did* father my unborn child, I feared their reaction. Complete shock. Intense dismay. Shame and heartbreak. That's the scene I knew awaited when I told them Isaac was not the father.

They loved Isaac. But how would they react to the shocking news? Isaac reassured me, "Don't worry. Just tell your parents I'm the father. That way, they'll be happy." And he often said, "I'll never leave you or the baby's side; I love you and always have." He continually reminded me, "A child is a blessing. And babe, I'm here forever."

As you can imagine, I hung on every word, my eyes welling with tears. "That's so sweet," I would reply, "but I can't do that. I don't want to lie. I'll tell my parents and the world my truth, and I love you more."

My mind would always think, "Who is this man? This is unreal; he really does love me." Thinking back, I can still picture that huge smile, such a bittersweet memory.

He continued telling me how happy he was to finally be with me, humbly sharing how he had a huge crush on me since high school, and even though I always had a boyfriend, he said he never gave up on trying to pursue me. I was beyond flattered and always thought he was very attractive, but in high school I had put him in the friend zone; I was totally clueless.

The more he talked, the more I fall in love with him. He was just so engaging, a breath of fresh air. Our relationship had been

2 – Still Unfulfilled

elevated to another level after that in-depth, heartfelt talk—and by "another level," I mean to physical intimacy. Yes, I always questioned being intimate with him while being pregnant with another man's child, and believe me, everyone around us felt the same way, but he didn't seem to care at all. He always told me how beautiful and special I was, reassuring me every chance he could that he had promised forever to never leave my side.

And then it was time: Isaac and I finally sat down with my parents to tell them the big secret. Picture this: I began sweating and stuttering, but before I could even begin to utter the words, "I'm pregnant," my parents quickly interrupted me.

"Alicia [that's my sister], told us this morning that she's concerned you're pregnant," my mom gushed, her voice quivering.

Alicia always made comments or references to me being pregnant, but I always denied it. I especially had no clue she would ever relay her worries to our parents. And although I was furious with my older sister, she'd really given me the push I needed because, without this open door, I honestly don't think I could have formed my lips into the correct words to tell my secret.

Shocked and incredulous, my parents asked, "Is it true you're pregnant?"

"Yes."

I kept looking intently at them, not at Isaac.

Turning to Isaac, they then asked in one breath, "Are you the baby's father? And what are your plans for Stacy and the baby?"

"Yes and no," he said back. "No, I'm not the father, but yes, I plan to be in the lives of Stacy and the baby forever." I began to laugh at the confusion etched on my parents' faces.

"Excuse me?" my mom asked, shaking her head.

I chimed in, telling my parents the whole detailed story about Josh and his decision to not be a part of our lives. And I gauged their reaction by my dad's clouded eyes and my mom's heavy sighs.

Quite disappointed but surprisingly supportive—that's how I would describe my parents' response. Both my parents were very strict, always stressing the importance of being married before having sex, so with these expectations I was quite intimidated to tell them everything. The hardest part of all was disappointing them. I only wanted to make them proud, but overall, they were very impressed by Isaac's courage and meekness. They were so relieved that he was committed to sticking around, and I was so thankful to have Isaac by my side.

As promised, Isaac made sure to accompany me to every single doctor's appointment; I was so grateful to not experience the pregnancy alone. My heart swelled with the overwhelming amount of love and support he gave me. He often placed his face on my stomach and talked directly to the baby in his own baby voice, which I found quite adorable.

Pouring my heart out in prayer, I continuously thanked God for this blessing He gave me called Isaac. I would cry refreshing tears, so grateful that God allowed me to know how it felt for my child to have a father and for me to have a loving partner through this life-altering experience. As the pregnancy continued to progress, I knew without a doubt that God had sent me an angel.

I was so thrilled to be having my baby now! The anxiety lifted, and I embraced being pregnant. As my baby bump grew larger, our love grew stronger, and we were able to deal with the negative reactions from friends and family regarding our untraditional relationship. I couldn't understand why people weren't happy for me, just excited I wasn't having to go through this pregnancy empty and alone. *"Aren't they happy I'm no longer depressed? Aren't they happy I have someone who loves me and my baby?"* I thought.

Shocked at not receiving loving support from my close loved ones, I saw all my fears about being judged become reality. No one could stop whispering about who really fathered my child, including all the sordid details about him. Plus, they all predicted

2 – Still Unfulfilled

Isaac would leave my side when the baby was born, and I have to admit, those thoughts kept plaguing me, too. Feeling like I was never "good enough," very insecure and anxious, I was convinced a happy ending would never happen for me. As I reflected on my childhood and every disappointment thereafter, I anticipated a devastating letdown.

At our last ultrasound appointment, we found out the baby's gender: a healthy, beautiful baby boy! As soon as Isaac heard "boy," he exclaimed, "I can't believe I'm having a son!" with excitement etched in every word.

I couldn't believe my ears. Did he just call the baby his son? Wow! *"This is unbelievable,"* I thought, *"He really considers this baby his son! Can I really have the family unit I've always yearned for?"* Isaac immediately asked if he could name him; he wanted our son to have his name! I couldn't be more overjoyed to see him so invested in our new family and to witness his genuine love for our unborn son. As I approached my ninth month of pregnancy, Isaac continued to show up at my family's home on a daily basis, never waning in his commitment.

With the baby's due date right around the corner, one Friday in late July began as usual—with me praying as I took a neighborhood walk; I wanted to help jumpstart my labor as much as possible. But as the day wore on, I realized Isaac hadn't yet called or shown up at the house. I made phone call after phone call, but still no call back or sign of Isaac. I began to worry because this behavior wasn't like him.

The next day came with still no word from Isaac, and I felt my heart sink deep in my chest: my worst fear was coming to pass! All the judgmental predictions of him leaving my side now became harsh reality. I thought I had prepared my heart for such disappointment, but the grief and sense of loss slammed into me. I knew it had all been too good to be true! There was no way I was capable of having a happily ever after. I wept relentlessly, hurt and broken by Isaac's sudden disappearance, but I soon knew I had to pull myself together; my son would arrive any day now, and I knew I must focus on doing this alone.

Saddened by Isaac's silence, my parents and siblings were now more supportive than ever. I could see their hurt for me as they desired only to keep me happy and healthy as we prepared for our new family addition. I knew one day I would be able to talk to Isaac again and thank him for standing by my side through this pregnancy. Although heartbroken, I still thanked God for giving me Isaac, even if for just a short while.

As I sat patiently awaiting this birth, the phone rang. It was Isaac! I was so ecstatic that he finally called, and while I was delighted to hear his voice, I didn't want him to know how upset I was. "How ya doin', Stacy?" he asked with raw concern in his voice.

"I'm fine," my voice responded, short and clipped.

"How's the baby?"

"Great."

As he could feel my despair through the phone, he began to tell me how sorry he was for his two-week disappearance.

"I love you and the baby so much," he said, "and you know that's my son ... little Isaac is my son." My heart skipped a few beats in the next brief silence.

Then he continued, explaining how he feared Josh would return to claim me and the baby and how he would be devastated if the baby were taken from his life. He said his friends and some family members had pelted him with their judgments and concerns of Josh's return, and he got scared. But then he had time to think long and hard, he said, and he realized he was here to stay.

"I'll never leave your side again, Stacy. I promise."

You can't imagine how relieved I felt in that moment.

"I forgive you," I said, reassuring him that Josh would never return. "And even if he ever does, you'll always be our son's father.

2 – Still Unfulfilled

Blood doesn't make someone a good father or define his role ... but love and commitment do."

The day finally arrived. As my contractions began coming in waves, very close together, I called Isaac to tell him it was time. He replied in a frenzy, rushing to pick me up, grabbing my bags, and carefully escorting me to his car. And then while everyone around me was in a panic, I became still for just a moment, taking it all in as my parents and I glanced at each other in amazement. A serene restfulness and inexpressible cheer came upon us, and then Isaac and I sped away in pursuit of the hospital. Though I was in excruciating pain, I also couldn't keep myself from smiling at him the entire car ride.

Ten hours of labor later, the time to push arrived, and with my mom and Isaac by my side coaching me along, our son finally greeted the world. Isaac, grinning through tears, proudly cut the umbilical cord just as I imagined he would. And there was our son ... so adorable and chunky. I couldn't stop gazing at this little blessing, and the instant love I felt for him was undeniable. In the calm atmosphere, I marveled, "This is really an unexplainable encounter with God; this is what His love tangibly feels like!"

Isaac stayed with the baby and me the entire night in the hospital, never leaving our side, and the next morning while Isaac and I held hands, admiring our new child, our nurse came in to have us sign the birth certificate. Isaac graciously took the pen in preparation to sign, and I thought, "This man never ceases to amaze me!" But I asked the nurse to give us a moment.

As she made her exit, Isaac turned to me in confusion, asking why the nurse had to leave. "Why didn't you let me sign the birth certificate?" he asked, his voice crestfallen.

I still hadn't shared with Isaac my concerns about our son being a "junior" and taking his last name without us being married. With Isaac's recent disappearance, my trust had grown shaky and I still feared him walking away. Yes, he was here now, but what if he decided to leave me and the baby again? With Isaac's name on the birth certificate, what would I do? First Josh? And now Isaac? *How would I explain this to my child?*

Isaac disappointedly stared into my eyes as I continued to tell him I would feel more comfortable with him signing the birth certificate after we were married. We had discussed marriage throughout our seventh-month relationship, both agreeing that's what we wanted, but we had no real plans in place. Isaac said he completely understood my hesitation, and in those few brief moments, we decided to name our new baby Jordan and temporarily give him my last name, leaving the father section blank with plans for Isaac to complete that information once we were married. Working out all these details together added another layer in the foundation of our relationship.

With the baby and I settled in at home with my parents and siblings, I received the around-the-clock support I needed, plus Isaac came every day to bond with Jordan. Astoundingly, baby Jordan actually resembled Isaac more than he did Josh! Can you even envision that miraculous move of God? My parents, always traditional in their views, surprisingly allowed Isaac to stay over some nights to help me with the baby. Yes, Isaac continued to receive special treatment from my parents as they were extremely touched by his love for their daughter and his willingness to assume responsibility in raising their new grandchild.

With great sarcasm, some family members would still continually ask me if I were sure who had fathered my child. They still couldn't believe Isaac would be this attentive to a child who wasn't biologically his. I would always reply by saying how much prayer works and ultimately ignoring their criticism.

2 – Still Unfulfilled

Deep down, I was so relieved Jordan didn't resemble Josh, who was naturally becoming a distant memory to me. I would even often forget that he is Jordan's biological father. Isaac was simply the missing piece to my puzzle. His unwavering commitment to our lives left many speechless, and after more time passed, most accepted that Isaac was here to stay, including myself. I never tried to find Josh to tell him when the baby was born; there was no word from him since our last toxic conversation, and I had no desire to inflict him with paying child support. From the earliest days, I felt no need to force him to "father" my unborn child, to provide for us or be a part of our lives in any way. I felt this immediately, well before running into Isaac at the mall. I think being a father should come willingly, without coercion, and Jordan already had a father: it was Isaac. A more loving and attentive father I could never hope to find.

Soon we were celebrating Jordan's five-month birthday, giggling and fawning over our sweet, happy baby. As Isaac and I were very much in love, I patiently awaited the big proposal, but when would it happen? With us both working full-time jobs, attempting to save money so we could finally move into our own place, we were both busy and a bit drained, and Isaac spent a huge amount of time at my house. With my parents definitely applying pressure, we talked about getting married soon, and, of course, my dad preferred this happen before we moved in together. Isaac had been an excellent provider for our little family, and I couldn't wait to be his wife, so what was he waiting for? Why hadn't he proposed yet? I hoped he wasn't having second thoughts.

Then on one particular day, Isaac was acting very strange, nervous and fidgety. I kept asking, "Is something wrong?" but he wouldn't give me a straight answer. We were sitting in my bedroom when he began to reluctantly speak, and then his eyes started watering. I was thinking, "Oh, no! He's trying to break up with me." But instead, he stood up straight and tall and then bent down on one knee.

"Stacy, will you do me the honor of being my wife?" he smiled.

I covered my mouth with my hand as tears fell down my face, at a loss for words, and my heart began beating 100 miles per hour.

"Yes, yes, I will marry you!" I replied trembling, and he placed the ring on my finger. Then we hugged each other so tightly, and I didn't want to let him go. I couldn't wrap my mind around what had just happened. I was in a dream. "Is this real?" my mind whirled. *"Is true happiness really possible for someone like me?"*

My wedding day finally arrived, and standing before the mirror in my wedding dress, I gazed in disbelief at the beautiful bride smiling back; I was trying to figure out how I had made it to that day. Jordan was nine months old, and we had planned this wedding in four short months with our parents' financial support—with a wedding party of 20 and a guest list of 300. It had been a rocky four months of planning, trying to blend our families and reach common ground in our religious beliefs. Yes, we hadn't talked that subject much, mostly because I kept putting it off and hoping it wouldn't matter for our future. Yet, we couldn't skirt the issue in planning the ceremony, and it had created some major tension between our families. Isaac's Muslim upbringing totally differed from my Christian one, forcing us to compromise in order to appease both families. I didn't realize how much our backgrounds would negatively impact us on our special day, wondering why we didn't dive into this topic earlier in our relationship.

The night before the wedding I could barely sleep. I had actually fallen asleep while praying, asking God to guide us throughout

2 – Still Unfulfilled

the wedding as I felt like something would surely go wrong. I was having so much anxiety, again feeling like it was all too good to be true, filled with a myriad of emotions. I was undeniably happy but also felt an uncontrollable sadness.

As I walked away from the mirror, I took a deep breath to prepare myself to walk with my father down the aisle. But everything I felt could go wrong went wrong. Isaac showed up an hour late, our minister showed up two hours late, and our family and friends were more than restless, which caused some tension-filled bickering. My mother, sisters, and best friends were right by my side, keeping me calm as I began to cry and ruin my perfectly applied makeup. I couldn't believe my perfect day wasn't so perfect after all, but as I looked over at Jordan in his little white tuxedo, all I wanted to do in that moment was marry the love of my life. I no longer cared about the drama around me. I instantly pulled myself together, and we were finally ready to start the wedding.

When my father saw me, he smiled, and then he lifted my veil and kissed me gently on my forehead. I can tell he was so proud to give me away to Isaac. The music played, and I took my first step, heading toward my groom, and my tears started flowing when our eyes connected from across the room. My heart fluttered more and more as I approached him. His teeth were gleaming white, his face was full of joy, and the way he passionately stared at me let me know how much he truly loved me. My father gave me away. I bashfully looked into Isaac's eyes as we said our vows. And I was thinking how handsome he was, asking myself, *"Is this really my husband? The little girl everyone gave up on is really getting married!"*

Isaac kissed me and we hugged so intensely, giving our deep emotions instant relief. We were officially husband and wife! As we headed out the doors holding hands, we heard the celebratory cheers in the background, and I realized I was really living out my fairytale. Everything I had ever dreamed of or prayed for was actually happening. Isaac made me so happy, and he loved me in a special kind of way I'd never felt before. It's like Isaac completed me. I wanted nothing more than to be his wife and raise our children. As long as I had Isaac by my side, everything would be okay, right? I married my best friend, my angel, but why—if I had it all—did I still feel so incomplete? What was missing?

> *But seek first the kingdom of God and his righteousness and all these things will be added to you. Therefore, do not be anxious about tomorrow, for tomorrow will be anxious for itself. Sufficient for the day is its own trouble.*
>
> **– Matthew 6:33-34**

3 – SHATTERED AND BROKEN

OUT ON THE TOWN TOGETHER, THE NIGHT shining starlit and gorgeous, Isaac and I walk back to our car hand-in-hand. We talk and laugh freely, enjoying each other's quick wit and latest parenting escapades. And then suddenly we see him: a homeless man, his eyes glassy and hair snarled, sitting on the sidewalk and giving us a half smile. While I stare at the man's weathered face, Isaac takes in the bigger picture, quickly noticing his bare feet. Without hesitation, Isaac quickly removes his shoes and graciously hands them to the homeless man.

"How can this be?" I'm thinking, my heart instantly moved with emotion. I know finding a man like Isaac is extremely rare, but his pure heart of compassion continues to surprise and amaze me. We rejoin hands and head toward the car, with Isaac now walking barefoot and carefree. Deep inside me, without reservation or pretense, I now feel something new ignite; feeling intensely loved and in love, I sense our relationship reaching the highest climax, our lives now bound together in admiration, purpose, and deepest passion.

Oh, friends, that memory still makes me smile, and I can see now how Isaac's character of integrity and selfless love were making my dreams come true. Being married was simply everything I imagined. I loved cooking, cleaning, and caring for my family. Yet just one aspect was missing: doing all this in our own home.

When we had moved in with my mother-in-law, Rosalyn, we were extremely grateful; she had offered us her home while we saved for our own place. But as one can imagine, this put a massive strain on our marriage as newlyweds. Living with his mom simply wasn't an easy transition. Certainly, witnessing Rosalyn's love and acceptance for her new grandson, Jordan, brought much comfort, but she only tolerated me. Isaac struggled to please both his mom and me around the clock, resulting in heartbreaking disagreements.

To my surprise and dejection, Isaac's extended family also struggled to welcome me in, which I could tell by their disapproving stares at every family function. At first, I thought maybe they were just standoffish because we had gotten married so quickly and no one had really had a chance to get to know me. Or maybe, I thought, they were being judgmental because of my back story with Jordan. For three months, the entire time we lived with Rosalyn, I witnessed Isaac's stress and overwhelmed demeanor, so when it was time to move out, we were ecstatic. We would finally live on our own with no interruptions. I was always hopeful that one day I would be accepted into his family organically—gradually and naturally. However, while Rosalyn loved Isaac and Jordan very much, she didn't believe any woman was good enough for her son, and she had no problem voicing her opinions every chance she got.

The moment we entered into our small, two-bedroom apartment, however, my contentment skyrocketed as my prayer life spiraled; I went from praying daily in my darkest hours to praying only sporadically. As God began answering my prayers, my need for His guidance and comfort seemed to lessen. We had little money, but for some reason it didn't matter as long as we had our growing family. And when we discovered I was pregnant again, this time with a baby girl, we were shocked but happy. Our new pregnancy was a huge surprise, but we couldn't be happier to have a boy and a girl just two years apart. Everything was perfect, just like I had always hoped and imagined.

I was extremely grateful for our basic lifestyle. I had become very comfortable working a minimum-wage job, with no real aspirations for myself professionally and simply wanting to support Isaac's dream of being an entrepreneur. Once Isaac's business took off, I reasoned, I could become a stay-at-home wife and mom. Until then, we had a great family plan, and we were right on track. I guess I was living out my dreams after all, but why did I still feel like something was missing? I still felt so incomplete, like something bad was going to happen.

"This is all too good to be true," I kept thinking. I really couldn't enjoy my good days because I continued to await my bad ones. I always cuddled with Isaac every chance I got, to the point I would make him crazy. I wanted to spend every waking moment with him, and when we were apart, I felt a deep emptiness. We spoke on the phone throughout the day, even while working. Isaac was very protective of Jordan and me, but then I felt a sudden need to protect *him*.

Waking up in bed with my amazing Isaac and beautiful baby Jordan was still unbelievable, giving me more security and assurance in my sixth month of pregnancy. During this time, Isaac began sharing with me a secret he had been holding in, one he now hesitantly related. At first, he stumbled a bit over his words, but then the details began spilling out as he shared how he had run into Josh at a local barber shop a few months back. My facial expression, he later said, was priceless. I couldn't believe it. I hadn't spoken to Josh since I had told him I was pregnant a couple of years prior.

"What did you talk about?" I asked quickly, my mind spinning.

"I told Josh that *I'm* Jordan's father and that I love him so much … and then I asked Josh if he had any thoughts about coming around. He said, 'No, not at all …. and besides, I'm married; I've never even told my wife or anyone that that baby ever existed.'"

Isaac continued telling Josh that he preferred he didn't come around at all because Jordan already had a father who'd never leave his side—and it was him. As Isaac shared this story, I began to think, *"Is it humanly possible to love him more than I do already?"*

The bond Isaac and Jordan shared was undeniable. Everyone just admired their love for one another, and I was so elated that Jordan had an incredible role model for a dad. In that split second, as Isaac shared his love and commitment to Jordan and me, it dawned on me that I wasn't the typical unmarried mother as everyone predicted. My life was turning out for the better, and they were all wrong about my future.

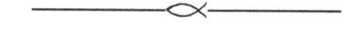

We were preparing for the birth of our baby girl, but on this particular night Isaac didn't return home at his expected time, so I began to worry. Surprisingly while I was praying, asking God to keep him safe from harm, I drifted off to sleep, only to awaken hours later. I had rolled over in bed, realizing Isaac hadn't returned home or returned my call. My initial worry quickly turned frantic as I immediately began to think the worst. First, I called his mom to see if he had stopped by there and perhaps had accidentally fallen asleep at her home. Rosalyn answered right away … and with great concern in her voice, she told me he had come by earlier

3 – Shattered And Broken

in the day but had left to head home. She rushed me off the phone to contact all his friends and cousins, trying to track him down. As Rosalyn made call after call, I began to contact the local hospital. Deep down, I knew something had happened, and I began to pace the apartment hallways, loudly crying out, "Where's my husband!?" My wailing even startled my neighbors.

When I called my parents to tell them Isaac was missing, my mother remained extremely calm, stating repeatedly, "Isaac is okay. Stacy, Isaac is okay." She continued to try to diffuse my intense anxiety, saying, "Stacy, you're eight months pregnant; you have to calm down for the sake of the baby." And I knew she was right, so I mustered all my courage and remained as calm as possible, racing to my phone every time it rang, hoping Isaac's voice would answer.

Hours passed and it was morning, with no sign of my husband. I fell to my knees, asking God to "please, please protect Isaac!" I continued weeping, crying out and asking God to please allow Isaac to meet his daughter.

"Please, don't let him be dead!" I pleaded. With no logical explanation, this same random thought would often enter my mind during the duration of my new pregnancy, fueling my desperate need to be close to him at all times and illuminating why I hated it when we were apart. In the following months, this cold, inexplicable feeling began to taunt me.

The phone rang, stifling my sobs. It was the local hospital. I answered in a panic and heard the man on the other end introduce himself as a chaplain. When I realized who he was, I nearly dropped the phone. In that moment, the entire world paused ... as I anticipated hearing the life-altering news tumble from his mouth. He began to tell me that Isaac had been in a horrible car accident but that he was alive and talking. Still, "You need to get to the hospital right away," he directed.

Thankfully, my sister Alicia had come by earlier that morning to comfort me and care for Jordan. I called Rosalyn to tell her what the chaplain had said, and then I darted to my car, rushing to the hospital to be by Isaac's side. As I approached the hospital emergency doors, fear and dread gripped me. I didn't know what to expect as my mind tried to deny the worst. Then, once I entered the emergency room and saw all those beds, injured and hurting people, and white-clad medical personnel, my heart sank into my stomach.

Peeking into the area where Isaac was located, I finally let out a gasp of relief. I saw him sitting up, talking and smiling with the nurses. When he saw me, his face lit up and his eyes immediately began to tear. I held him so tight, silently thanking God for keeping him safe. I was so happy he was alive and well.

Isaac walked away from that horrific accident with only a few stitches, and after seeing his car, I knew God had been merciful in saving my husband; I knew it had been a miracle.

After this incident, my anxiety increased. My worries for Isaac's safety were even more intense than before, but now our daughter had been born and we had much to celebrate. After praying for God to help me, I stopped focusing on the accident and all the "what ifs" and started appreciating each moment we all had together.

When Isaac first laid eyes on our daughter, Haniyyah, I felt instant thankfulness. I felt God had answered my prayers and gifted Isaac with the opportunity to meet his daughter. And as Isaac started a new job managing his cousin's new business, a position he viewed with much excitement, we really began seeing our lives returning to normal. We were finally able to move into a new condo with more amenities, and Isaac was so proud to relocate his family into a more upscale environment. After Haniyyah's birth, I didn't return to work but was finally that stay-at-home wife and mom I had always longed to be. Isaac and I felt our time had finally arrived.

3 – Shattered And Broken

I even started to pray more, just like I had in the past, trusting God with our future. Isaac and I were in search of a church home, and even though Isaac was born into a Muslim family, he was becoming more open to my Christian upbringing. Before our marriage, we hadn't really thought through the ramifications of our different spiritual backgrounds, and in those early days as newlyweds we saw the friction it could cause—making us realize the importance of being equally yoked spiritually. We discovered it really had potential to create an obstacle in our marriage's longevity and how we raised our children. Thankfully, Isaac was very compromising and easy to love. He always respected my views, and I was supportive of him as well.

As Haniyyah's early months began slipping by, Isaac seemed to be at great peace with life, in his sweet spot, you could say. He was always a jokester and pleasant to be around, but he was even more fun and amiable than usual. He even began singing tunes around the house for no apparent reason. We were only in our new place for a couple of weeks when one evening Isaac shocked me by not only putting both Jordan and Haniyyah's new beds and dressers together without my assistance, a project I was desperately dreading, but he also took the time to organize their closets and drawers. Very thoughtful, I mused. Even though he worked longed hours and came home tired, he consistently took the time to jump in wholeheartedly as a loving, hands-on dad with our children and to assist with the upkeep of our home.

One Sunday morning around 9 a.m., I awoke to feed four-month-old Haniyyah and realized Isaac had already awakened, gotten dressed, and left without my knowledge. I wasn't concerned, thinking he may have run off to grab breakfast or plan a special surprise for me. Oftentimes he would "awe" me with flowers or gifts, a huge part of his personality.

When Isaac returned, I noticed he looked quite sharp, and I quickly asked, "Hey, Isaac, where'd you go?"

He smiled and said, "I went to church this morning."

Taken aback, I said, "You went without me and the kids? We were planning to go together."

"I know," he replied, "but you all were sleeping so peacefully. I didn't want to disturb you, and I really wanted to go this morning."

Wow! I couldn't believe it. He was actually on fire to go to church! His attendance had become vital to him in recent weeks, and he continued to tell me the exciting details of the service. "Next Sunday, we'll all go, and I'm thinking this is the church I'd like for us to join as new members."

Just wow! I was speechless with joy.

The following Saturday arrived, and Isaac and I were planning to attend church as a family the next morning. But then I realized I didn't have any church attire that fit after recently having a baby. So, Isaac said he'd stay home with the kids while I ran to the mall. Just before I stepped out, Isaac said his mom was going to watch the kids instead; he had forgotten about plans he'd already made to meet up with his friend Shawn.

Once Rosalyn arrived, I headed to the mall, excited at the prospect of buying something new for church the next day. It was such a beautiful Saturday afternoon, and I knew I could take my time without having to race back home. I felt such peace and was anticipating my rare time alone, extremely grateful for the chance to shop and walk the mall. But when I walked through the mall doors, I felt it happening again: without warning, a pressing burden began to overtake me.

3 – Shattered And Broken

On the spot, I called Rosalyn to check on the children. I then called to check on Isaac. Even though everyone was okay, I still wrapped up my shopping early and headed home, listening to inspirational music on the car radio with the windows down. The music brought me sudden calmness, and I called Isaac to let him know I would be home shortly.

"Me, too," he said, "I'm right up the street. And hey, I'm looking forward to us going to church tomorrow."

"Me, too, babe. Me, too." And then I hung up. I pulled up in front of our condo to wait for him, but after a few minutes, I decided to head inside.

———⊂✕⊃———

Hearing Rosalyn so full of laughter with her grandchildren, I called out to her, "I'm back!"

"So quickly?" she asked.

"Yes, Isaac will be hear any second. Do you want to wait for him?"

"Sure," she replied.

I heard Jordan jumping up and down on our bed, repeatedly yelling, "Daddy's home! Daddy's home!"

I looked out our bedroom window and saw his parked car, so I said to Rosalyn, "Isaac's here." Rosalyn and I continued chatting, awaiting Isaac's entry, but after several minutes had passed, we noticed Isaac never entered the condo. Rosalyn and I began to laugh, saying he's probably just sitting in the car listening to music. I returned back to my bedroom window, and saw the car was still parked.

I decided to call him on his cell phone but no answer, so I figured I would surprise him at his car door. But when I stepped up to the driver's side, no one was there. Then subconsciously, I looked down at the ground for any evidence of blood. Why did I do that? Until this day, I have no idea. I then looked around our condominium complex and noticed fire trucks a few buildings over. Although I saw no sign of Isaac, I walked back in to tell Rosalyn that Isaac may be talking to the firemen to see what's going on in the neighborhood; he was that type of gentleman. Rosalyn agreed and decided to head out herself.

She said, "Stacy, tell Isaac to just give me a call when he gets in the door."

I laughed and said, "Okay." Moments after Rosalyn pulled off, I still felt unsettled and began calling Isaac's number repeatedly, again and again … and still no answer.

My stomach began to knot up. Something must be wrong! Where could he have gone? I picked up my phone again and began calling him once more, hoping he would answer this time. Finally, someone answered, but the voice on the other end wasn't Isaac's.

I demanded, "Who is this?"

He said, "This is the local police. Who are you?" The officer asked me to immediately identify myself.

Trembling in fear, my voice yelled out, "I'm his wife! Where's my husband? Why do you have his phone?"

The officer paused and said, "Ma'am, I don't know how to say this …" It seemed like hours passed as I waited for him to continue.

"Your husband has been shot in the chest and is being rushed in an ambulance to the nearby hospital."

I cried out to the officer, *"What happened? Who did this? IS HE ALIVE?"*

The officer replied, "I don't know; you need to head to the hospital."

I hang up the phone … the room is spinning … I can't move my feet … I fall to my knees. I cry out to God in complete despair. "God, please don't let him die! God, please let me see him and tell him I love him before he dies! God, please let me tell him goodbye!" I remember our conversation an hour prior and that I didn't tell him goodbye or that I loved him.

3 – Shattered And Broken

"God, please don't let him die! What would I do without him? The kids are only two years old and four months old. He can't die! He can't die! God, I'm so sorry for anything I have ever done! Please, don't let my husband die …"

―――――∝―――――

The Lord is close to the brokenhearted and saves those crushed in spirit.

– Psalm 34:18

4 – LOST AND REMOVED

MY MIND IS SPINNING, REELING IN DENIAL that anything so life-shattering and catastrophic in my world could ever be happening.

"Isaac is supposed to be here," I'm thinking, "He's supposed to attend Jordan's first football game and escort Haniyyah to her first daddy-daughter dance. We're planning to purchase our first home together, and our life is so beautiful!

"How can this be?" I plead with God, "What wrong have I committed to deserve for my only true love to die? What will I tell our children?"

As I speed to the hospital to be by my husband's side, I repeatedly cry out each of these questions encircling my mind. The car ride seems so familiar; realizing I had taken this same route six months before, I now once again feel the same pain and fear of losing Isaac—identical tragedies!

"My God," I implore, "please perform another miracle!" That's my ongoing lament—the words welling up from the anguished pain in my chest—my desperate prayer until I walk through those emergency room doors.

As I approach my weeping mother, I wait for her to say the words, "Isaac is dead." My God, I didn't make it in time to tell him goodbye!

As tears pour out of my eyes and my limp body falls into my mother's arms, she whispers in my ear, "Stacy, Isaac is in surgery; he's not dead! He may be able to pull through."

---------∝---------

I simply couldn't believe what I was hearing. Even today, I can still remember that elation as I began to cry out with relief, and then all my family members locked hands, passionately praying for God to heal Isaac. The waiting room was spinning, my knees were trembling, and the surgery seemed to be going on for hours; every second felt like an eternity.

Finally, Isaac's surgeon appeared. He approached me with such hesitation, giving me a look of uncertainty that squeezed the last drop of hope from my heart. I stared at the floor the entire time, unable to face the horrific news, the dread-filled words beginning to flow from his mouth. He said, "Mrs. Thomas?"

I looked up and whispered, "Yes."

Then his serious expression was replaced with a smile. He said, "Isaac will make a full recovery; he was shot in the back, but the bullet missed every major organ and his spine. We only had to remove a small portion of his spleen."

Did he just say Isaac will live? Am I dreaming? My mind was silently trying to grasp those words.

The meaning suddenly sinking in, I literally jumped for joy, hugging the surgeon so tightly. The entire waiting room celebrated and rejoiced; our tears of sorrow instantly became tears of joy. I was so incredibly thankful that God had saved my husband again.

I was thinking, *God, thank you for hearing my cries! You answered me again!*

The surgeon said, "Follow me, Mrs. Thomas, Isaac wants to see you."

4 – Lost And Removed

"Are you serious?" I stammered. "You mean he's awake? He can talk?"

The doctor smiled and responded, "Yes, he's a little groggy, but he's alert."

This seemed so surreal. I was still a bit skeptical but also enormously excited for my eyes to connect with Isaac's, to be able to hold him once again when, just moments earlier, I had thought it humanly impossible for him to recover from such a severe wound.

The doors of his hospital room swung open, and there he was, lying quietly in a bed, sleeping so peacefully.

I said, "Isaac, it's me. I'm here."

As I reached out to hold his blood-stained hand, his eyes popped open with a look of great tenderness and relief. When our gazes locked together, his tears started to fall. He was so happy to see me, and I held his face with both hands and uncontrollably kissed him all over his cheeks. I was actually able to hold and touch him. I wasn't dreaming!

He slowly asked, "Stacy, are you okay?" I couldn't believe he was concerned about my well-being after he had almost lost his life.

I said, "I'm okay now that I know you're okay."

He said, "What happened? How did I get here? ... Who would want to shoot me?"

I said, "Baby, you're safe now. Everything will be okay; just relax, and I'll explain everything later."

As I sat for the next many hours and all through the night in that hard hospital chair, watching my husband recovering from a gunshot wound and hooked up to countless machines, I couldn't help but question God. How had we gotten to this place? I was overwhelmed with emotions, extremely grateful he survived yet saddened by the senseless act of violence.

Isaac had now had two very recent brushes with death. Why was tragedy surrounding my sweet Isaac? I contemplated everything.

Overall, he was alive and well. I was ecstatic he was here with me, smiling as we discussed him coming home from the hospital soon. Although we were both amazed by God's miraculous saving power, I was still in disbelief, restless and full of anxiety. Feeling so unsettled and uneasy, I began to anticipate more bad news, sensing that Isaac's impeccable health report was all too good to be true.

The next morning it was time for me to leave Isaac's side; I needed to head home to refresh myself and check on our children. I dreaded leaving Isaac. In fact, I refused to leave until his mom, Rosalyn, came to relieve me. I said, "Isaac, I'm leaving now to check on the kids, but I'll be back in a couple of hours, and your mom is here."

He said, "Stacy, I'm okay, stop worrying. Please kiss the kids for me and tell them I'll be home soon. I love you."

I said, "I love you, too."

We kissed. And then as I walked away, heading toward the door, I stopped suddenly, and looking back over my shoulder, I waved good-bye. He smiled and softly said, "Good-bye."

I shuffled toward my cousin Lori's car, where she patiently waited to take me to the home of my parents who were safely keeping our children. The entire car ride there I felt nauseous. My cousin attempted to carry on a conversation in order to ease my nerves, but I couldn't stop feeling regretful about leaving Isaac.

Just moments after arriving at my parents' home and kissing our children, I felt a sudden need to check on Isaac's condition. I called the nurses' station, but there was no answer. I frantically approached my cousin Lori, telling her we needed to go back to the hospital right away. She said, "Stacy, we just got here."

I said, "I don't care; we must go back now! Something is wrong with Isaac."

She asked, "How do you know?"

I said, "I can feel it."

4 – Lost And Removed

She gave me a strange look, as if I had lost my mind. I knew deep down inside something was wrong. I felt like a piece of me was slowly escaping my body, leaving behind a strong presence of grief. My family was trying to convince me otherwise, repeatedly saying, "Stacy, you were just with Isaac thirty minutes ago. He was up and talking. What makes you believe something has happened?"

I ignored them, and racing back into my cousin's car, I pleaded with her to "hurry up, please hurry! I have to get to Isaac before it's too late.!" Lori was very confused but did exactly what I asked, driving me quickly back to the hospital, safe and sound. I leapt from the car and raced through the emergency room doors but was immediately stopped by hospital security. The security guard said, "Ma'am, you can't go this way. You have to go around to the main hospital entrance."

"I have to walk all the way to the other side of the hospital?" Both frantic and frustrated, I pleaded, "That will take way too long! Sir, my husband needs me, something has happened!"

He said, "Ma'am, I'm sorry, but you can't go this way."

I ran out the emergency room doors, and by this time, Lori had driven off. I ran as fast I could to the other side of the hospital, which seemed like miles. I rushed up to the front desk at the main entrance completely breathless, and once I gave my identity, I was finally allowed up. I ran to the elevator, which was taking forever, and I knew something was wrong—as if something were preventing me from getting to Isaac.

When I stepped off the elevator, I noticed an awkward quietness among several family members there as they lingered in the waiting room. I abruptly said, "What's wrong with Isaac?" No one replied, and as their heads hung low, I began to become more and more frightened, and I turned to rush back to Isaac's room. That's when I saw from a distance a crew of nurses, all scurrying in and out of his room, and I yelled down the hallway, "What happened to my husband?" When I finally stepped through his room door, I saw him sitting up in a chair. Rosalyn was crying out and holding him, and I immediately exclaimed to her, "What happened?" I began to hold him as well, saying, "Baby, what's wrong? Tell me what's wrong."

His eyes rolled to the back of his head and he was losing air in his body as he reached out to us for help. I felt so helpless. I looked at the nurses in such agony, begging them to do something. The nurses forced me and Rosalyn out of the room, and I heard the words "Code Blue" over the hospital intercom.

"This can't be happening again," I kept repeating as my distraught body leaned into family members. "He was just healthy and well!" I yelled out. "Why, God? Why?"

After minutes passed with no update on Isaac's current condition, the doctor finally came out and grabbed my arm, leading me back to Isaac's room. He told me Isaac had gone into cardiac arrest but was still alive, and they were running tests to evaluate any form of brain activity. I didn't know what to expect when I saw him; I didn't know how much more I could emotionally endure. When I saw Isaac, he looked like a totally different person. His eyes covered with white spots, I knew at that moment he was gone. Still, I was hopelessly desperate for him to pull through. I threw myself across his body, weeping and crying out, begging him to fight, telling him, "You can't die, baby; if you die, I won't be able to survive without you!"

As I started asking God to save Isaac one more time and glimpsing his face once more, I suddenly felt myself unable to breathe, and I quickly left his room. I couldn't bear to see my love in that condition. Stumbling into the hallway, I was broken to pieces. When I returned back to the waiting area, I once more found myself in a chair, and that's where the family and I sat for hours, anticipating the results of Isaac's tests. These tests would determine if Isaac would live or die.

The family started praying for another miracle; we were all so shocked by this traumatic turn of events. After some heartrending

4 – Lost And Removed

petitions to God, I felt the strength to go back into Isaac's room and face him, and just then an instant, fearless peace took over my soul. I stopped weeping, and when I walked into Isaac's room, I saw a peace come over him as well. He was beginning to look like himself again. I was praying and pleading for God to keep him, and I was begging him to fight to stay because I couldn't grasp the thought of life without him. In that moment, I began to kiss his lips and cheeks, and with my forehead attached to his, I let out a big sigh and said, "Isaac, I'll be okay. You can go be with God now; don't worry about me and the kids. We'll be okay."

I couldn't believe what God allowed to spill from my lips. I got up and stared out the window into the sunny sky, feeling an instant comfort. When I looked over at Isaac, I was surprised to see tears rolling down his face. I knew he had heard every word I said. I returned back to the waiting room, and when the doctor returned to give the family the test results, I had an ounce of hope; I knew God could save Isaac again. I looked into the doctor's eyes, feeling more than equipped for the outcome of the tests. But the doctor said, *"I'm sorry, Mrs. Thomas, Isaac is dead. There's no brain activity. I'm so sorry."*

I let out the deepest cry of sorrow, and then slumping to the floor, I passed out from a surge of anxiety, somehow hoping to die right along with my husband. I remember waking up in a hospital bed with an oxygen mask over my mouth, barely able to breathe on my own, seeing my mother crying over me and my father standing behind her in complete despair. I didn't know what had happened. I felt a bit of relief as I thought that Isaac dying had all been a nightmare.

I said, "Mom, is it true? Is Isaac really gone?"
She said "Yes."
I said, "No, Mom, please tell me it's all a bad dream."
She said, "It's true, Stacy. Isaac didn't make it."

I said, "Mom ... Dad ... just let me lie here and die. I can't go on with life without Isaac. Can you please raise our children? Please just let me die."

My mom cried out, and my father turned his face away.

"Stacy, you're strong," my mom soothed in her calming voice. "God will get you through this, trust me. You're a fighter."

But I disagreed with her. I wasn't a fighter; Isaac was my strength. I lay there in the hospital bed, hopelessly devastated, and then my intense heartache turned to anger. I began to lash out at my parents and the hospital staff, no longer desiring their comfort. I only wanted my husband back, and there was nothing they could say or do to ease my pain.

After a few hours passed, it was now time to release me from the hospital. But I was unable to stand up on my own two feet, and I begged my parents to please allow me to stay in the hospital just a little longer.

I can't bear facing the harsh reality of losing my one true love ...

... the harsh reality of losing my only friend ...

... the harsh reality that the only man who truly loved all of me was now dead ...

... the harsh reality that the angel God sent into my life in my darkest hours was now gone ...

I can't bear facing the harsh reality of being a widow at the young age of 23, with two babies to raise all alone ...

... and now our children will never know how amazing their father was.

These repetitive, disjointed thoughts raced through my mind as the nurses attempted to lift my limp body and set me into a wheelchair. Then my mother began to push me out the hospital's main entrance, and I spent that very long ride to my parents' car with my hands covering my entire face, crying uncontrollably. I could only think back to the moment when I met Isaac at the mall, realizing it was in the same place where I had met Josh.

"What does this all mean?" I wondered. While Josh had disposed of me and Jordan, Isaac had lovingly embraced us—but he was now dead!

Why would God bless me with a phenomenal husband and then take him?

Why would God bless Jordan with an extraordinary father but then take him?

Why would God bless five-month-old Haniyyah with a father she would never know? This all made no sense to me. I couldn't fathom such devastation.

I guess it was all too good to be true after all. A person like me would never be worthy enough to have a happy ending. Isaac promised he would never leave me, and this was now the only promise to me he ever broke. And I was extremely angry with him! How could he leave me? *Isaac made me love him and now he has died*, I thought over and over.

When I arrived at the car to climb in, I instantly knew a large part of my heart was vanquished, and the once hopeful young lady was no longer there. In an instant my goals, my dreams, my desires, and the willingness to live was snatched from me. What could my future possibly hold now that Isaac was dead?

He was my other half, he made me laugh when I was sad, he made me look forward to seeing another day ... he made life worth living.

In that split second, the thought of me taking my own life seemed the only answer. I loved my children very much, but how could I raise them if I were empty? How can I be good mother if my heart were shattered into pieces? I had nothing else to offer. Nothing humanly possible would be able to mend my broken heart. The destruction I endured would permanently change me for the rest of my life.

It would take a miracle to save me!

__Though he may stumble, he will not fall, for the Lord upholds him with His hand.__

— Psalm 37:24

5 – MISPLACED AND DAZED

THIS WAS AN OUT-OF-BODY EXPERIENCE. I felt like I was watching myself move without emotion, talk without feeling, interact with no joy or passion in any part of my soul. I knew I was alive but felt dead inside: I had no purpose to live anymore. "How can anyone find happiness again after such trauma?" Thoughts of despair enveloped my heart ... "Does God still love me? .... Am I really this undeserving of happiness?"

As we pull up to my parents' house, I realize there's no possible way for me to survive this tragedy. I crawl into my sister's bed, desperately wanting to sleep my pain away, with no desire to ever wake up again. I ask God repeatedly to please allow me to die a peaceful death in my sleep—suicide is not an option. But when the sun rises the next morning, I open my eyes ... reeling with anger! I had pleaded with God to please let me die ... but I'm still here.

"Can I please go to heaven to be with Isaac, Lord? After all You've done, I'm begging you, Jesus!"

I'm breathless, unable to move, unable to get out of bed to even use the restroom. My body—lifeless. I lay there in bed staring up at the ceiling, incapable of praying and wallowing in anger at God for allowing this to happen.

Suddenly, there's a knock at the door ... it's my mother.

"Stacy, are you okay?" she asks, pushing the door open a crack.

I reply with silence.

She says, "Well, I can't even imagine how you must feel, but you have to eat."

As she steps into the room, I speak slowly, telling her, "I'll never eat again; I have no appetite." Looking into her eyes as I sit up in bed, I say that I'm serious about wanting to die, wanting her and my father to raise my children. I'm completely shattered, unrepairable, with no way humanly possible to be put back together. I'll never heal from this type of a loss—never!

I know I'll never forget my mother's reply ...

She says, "Stacy, you will live, and you will be happy again, and you will raise your two beautiful children." But her response goes in one ear and out the other, leaving no impression on my mind or heart. The pain crushes and consumes me.

But then ... it was time to make funeral arrangements.

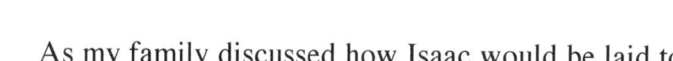

As my family discussed how Isaac would be laid to rest, I sat there in complete silence, with no desire to engage in such foolish talk. I still couldn't wrap my mind around his death ... and then my family began to ask me questions about Isaac's finances.

They couldn't believe that Isaac and I had no savings account, Isaac didn't have a life insurance policy, and I was now in financial despair.

Isaac was the bread winner; I was an at-home mom. I never wanted to think of Isaac dying, and we never took the time to create life insurance policies. But the unimaginable did happen. As I sat at the funeral in a daze, I laid on my father's shoulder, counting down the minutes, then seconds.

Thinking to myself that God really must have His hand on me, or else how am I able to sit here so peacefully while Isaac is lying there in that casket?

5 – Misplaced And Dazed

Is this real? This can't be ... he has to wake up and say, "Stacy, this is all a big joke, I'm not really dead." This has to be a really bad dream ... or else how did I get here?

I replayed this question over and over again in my head. I was in utter disbelief! I recall an enormous amount of people lined up inside the church to share their kind thoughts and love for Isaac, and I realized that he didn't touch only my life but also the lives of so many.

Then I stand there on the grass as the casket begins to lower into the grave. I'm saying to myself, "I should jump in and go with him," but my feet remain plastered to the ground and I can't move. But then a memory begins to surface ...

I remembered my cry out to God just a week before, asking Him to allow me to tell Isaac goodbye ... and God had actually answered my prayer. He gave me the miraculous gift of saying goodbye. I realized that many haven't been given such a blessed opportunity.

"Perhaps God is still here with me and hasn't left my side," I mumble to myself. Even though my eyes can see it's a sunny day outside, my insides see only darkness and gloom ... still, many friends and family are here to comfort and hold me—telling me over and over "I'm here for you" and "This, too, shall pass. We are praying for you, Stacy, and the kids." But those words are falling on deaf ears—even though so many surround me with love, I feel so alone and empty ... a very familiar place I'm becoming accustom to.

---———∝———---

It had been weeks since the funeral passed, and I was still unable to eat without others' assistance, bathe myself, or hold six-month-old Haniyyah. I couldn't do these things because then I would be living, something I had no desire to do. I was severely depressed.

I recall having harsh anxiety attacks and passing out, with family having to call in the paramedics in order for me to receive oxygen. I found comfort in taking prescription drugs, forcing myself to sleep through the excruciating pain ... but then it was time for me to move out of the home that Isaac and I had come to with such expectation.

I stood there now in our empty living room, thinking that, just a few weeks prior, Isaac and I with the kids were moving into this new condominium ... and now I was moving back in with my parents with my two babies. Back to where it all started? How quickly your plans can change! My life reversed within a blink of an eye. I still had no idea why Isaac was gunned down in the front of our home, so I found myself becoming paranoid. My anxiety heightened ... did someone want to harm me as well? Was someone targeting our little family?

Isaac was a hard-working man; everyone loved him. So, I couldn't wrap my mind around why anyone would want to hurt him.

I spoke with the detectives on countless occasions to try to get some answers. The police seemed to think it was a case of mistaken identity and that the shooter had no intention of targeting Isaac. He was just at the wrong place at the wrong time! *"How unfair is that?"* I thought. *"An innocent life has been taken! A senseless murder!?"*

As this new information surfaced, it only made me angrier and sadder. I tried to pull myself together for my children, knowing they needed me more now than ever, but my heart was constantly throbbing with indescribable pain. I remember saying this prayer almost every night: "God, please, please comfort my aching heart ... in Jesus name." And the moment I would utter that prayer, I would feel instant relief, a new kind of peace.

5 – Misplaced And Dazed

I had so much support, with my mother taking weeks off from work to care for my children through my bedridden days, but it was now time for her to head back to work. I noticed that the phone calls to check on my well-being began to cease, and I was left to pick up the broken pieces of my life.

But the next part of this tragedy still shocks me: I began learning that some of my family and friends were creating their own versions of Isaac's death. They were even making up false stories pertaining to our marriage, accusing Isaac of being unfaithful to me. I couldn't believe my ears ... that a handful of my loved ones were actually spreading rumors about my marriage after such a traumatizing, life-altering experience.

It seemed like they wanted to distort my loving memories of Isaac, but no one could convince me of such absurdity.

I started to believe that people were actually happy to see me pained, like they didn't want me to have my happily ever after. Why would anyone treat someone this way? *Don't they know I'm severely saddened? That I don't even love myself?* I felt like I was gazing down from a cliff's edge ... *Do they want me to just tumble over and die? How can they kick me while I'm down?*

After weeks in bed, I realized that I had to push through the pain. I was either going to die, too, or fight to live. Each day began to get better, the pain becoming more tolerable. Even though at times I was still unable to pray for myself, I knew someone *had* to be praying for me—because there was something, Someone, pulling me out of this dark place. I found myself driving for hours and hours with nowhere to go, no destination and no purpose. My thoughts on these drives would continue besieging me as I pondered my life's story, the one I had subconsciously penned as "My Only Desire Is to Be Isaac's Wife and Raise Our Children Together" ... but now that Isaac was dead, what would I do? How would I be able to raise these children alone?

I had no passion and no will. I didn't feel like *me* anymore; the spark of light that everyone loved so much was now gone forever, my future a foggy blur. During those weeks and months of pondering, I took that night drive often.

My family thought it would be a great idea for me to start grief counseling; they were still very concerned about my healing process. My mother knew that the kids and I would be moving out soon, and she wanted to make sure I was handling my grief in a healthy way. My parents even arranged for prayer warriors to come over to the house to pray with me. I remember just sitting there, crying tears of despair while they prayed, remaining ever hopeful that one day this weight on my heart would be lifted.

And I actually couldn't wait to finally start grief therapy—I was so desperately searching for relief from the ongoing pain. As I sat across from the grief counselor, she began to ask me a load of questions about Isaac. *How had we met? Tell me about your first kiss?* She wanted to learn more and more about our love story. And I felt an instant peace just talking about the love we shared. With tears rippling down my cheeks as I began to answer her difficult questions, she shared with me the five stages of grief: *denial, anger, bargaining, depression, and acceptance*. I returned to the grief counseling sessions weekly in hopes that I could finally get to a place of acceptance. After some time passed, however, the cost of these appointments began to weigh on my budget and I had to stop going; I was on a fixed income, attempting to save money and prepare for my children and I to finally leave my parents' home. As much as I appreciated my parents' support, I was ready to face my reality of being a 24-year-old widow with two children alone.

My parents pleaded for us to stay a little longer, but I knew this was the step I needed to take. I even started hanging out with my friends again on occasion ... maybe this was just what I needed to help move past the tragedy? Several months had passed, I was still having sleepless nights, experiencing nightmare after nightmare yet putting on a brave face for my children and others.

My children brought me great joy, but I was still completely empty. I tried to stay positive and even attempted to say quick prayers from time to time, but nothing seemed to penetrate the sadness. I was still hurting so much inside ... with no one able to understand me or relate to me anymore. I would call my family and friends, often attempting to receive the comfort of encouraging words so they could make my pain go away ... but they seemed to be speechless and helpless, with no words left to say.

Nothing I attempted to bring about healing was working, and I hated being alone. When I would roll over in bed every morning and realize once more that Isaac was no longer there, a fresh dread would pierce my heart. I missed Isaac desperately, but he was now gone. *Maybe I should listen to my friends and start dating? I'm only 24 years old, in need of a companion. Maybe if I have a boyfriend it will help fill this void in my heart? Maybe a boyfriend is the answer to all my troubles? If I can share my bed with a man, maybe I won't feel Isaac's absence?*

―――⊂✕⊃―――

> **Be strong and courageous, do not be afraid or tremble in dread before them, for it is the LORD your God who goes with you. He will not fail you or abandon you.**
>
> *– Deuteronomy 31:6*

6 – THE SEARCH CONTINUES

―――――∝―――――

TWO YEARS AGO, NO ONE COULD HAVE TOLD me that I would be preparing to go on a date. I want nothing more than to still be married to Isaac and absorbed in our love. But I have no choice; I feel like I'm being forced to date, pushed to move on with life. Maybe I will like this man? Maybe he can bring me happiness? Maybe having a new boyfriend will mend my broken heart? With no peace in sight, my heart and mind engaged in a tug of war, my soul aching, I find myself trekking down this broken road in a desperate search for happiness again.

As I sat across from my date, Todd, I realized how completely opposite he was from Isaac. He proceeded to ask me questions: "What I was looking for in a man? Was I opened to being in a relationship?" He was very interested in getting to know me.

Before I could even respond, I began to think, *"Will I ever love in the same way or capacity again? Because when we connect eyes, I feel no butterflies, no instant connection. He's very attractive, there's great conversation, but I'm not impressed. Maybe because I keep comparing him to Isaac, it just means I wish Isaac were alive. How amazing it would be if it were Isaac sitting across from me and not Todd!"*

I finally began to tell him that I was a widow—that my husband had been murdered the year before. The entire date I discussed the details of Isaac's death and our marital bliss. I proceeded to tell him that I wasn't looking for anything serious. I was now just interested in being friends. Todd seemed to be compassionate toward Isaac's tragic death, and after our first date, I was shocked to learn he wanted a second. I agreed ... and then a third date followed.

Todd's presence gave me something to look forward to. He was a placeholder, you could say. He gave me the attention my soul so desperately demanded.

And now my insides wince a little when I say this: our dates eventually turned into a three-year relationship. You see, I struggled with loving him the entire time. I mean, I loved him, but I didn't know how to be "in love" anymore. Half of my heart was missing and I didn't know where to find it.

But how was this possible? Why did I still feel a heavy emptiness? I thought if I had a boyfriend, it would help me to forget about Isaac, about the searing loss. I thought if I replaced Isaac with Todd, it would be the quick fix I needed to end my sleepless, lonely nights. I was in a committed, intimate relationship and wasn't physically alone, but I lacked fulfillment. I never stopped dreaming about Isaac; I continued to wake up from sleep gasping for air, with my pillow soaked with tears. When I would look to my right, Todd would be there. He was lying right beside me, but my heart still longed for Isaac. I started to wonder, *"Will I ever be normal again? Will I ever be a wife again?"* I was so hopeful that my children could one day have the amazing stepfather they deeply deserved.

"I know I may not love Todd now the way he loves me, but maybe that can change in the future. I guess I should just go ahead and marry him so I'll no longer have to fornicate." I was a ball of confusion, still fighting to pray and read my Bible occasionally.

I asked God, "Is it possible for me to be in love again if I'm still in love with Isaac? Is my heart capable of loving more than one person at the same time?"

6 – The Search Continues

---∝---

I waited and waited for God's response. I wanted to please God; and I wanted my family dynamic again. I figured I would just move forward with my plans of moving in with Todd while I waited for God to answer. I was hopeful that my heart would shift and love again. *"It's possible for me to truly love Todd eventually ...right?"*

Plus, Todd had it all together. He was successful and stable. I was still working odd jobs to care for Jordan and Haniyyah, so I thought it might be a great idea to consider marriage after all. I was stuck in my own internal struggle, with no clue who I was anymore, no career goals before me, no ability to see beyond my present pain. So, I decided to talk to Todd about my struggles; I was finally ready to let him in.

I told him that I was having a hard time accepting my circumstances. I said I was indecisive about my professional goals and literally having to start my life over. "I'm lost," I shared.

His reply shocked me. He basically said, "Stacy, you know I can have any other woman I want, but I choose *you*—I want *you*!"

However, before anyone begins to think Todd was a caring, doting partner, think again: there was another side to the story. (Did you catch the arrogance in his last remark?) While I *wished* for him to love me, his tone was always filled with pride—a super-sized ego making me feel like I was privileged to receive his attention.

He was definitely not impressed by my lack of ambition or lack of income either. "It's actually a turn off," he continued to say. "If you want a future with me, you'll need to get your business in order quickly."

Wow. How could he say this, knowing what I had been through? I didn't think I could feel lower than I already did, but a part of me agreed with him. I didn't feel like I was good enough for him—or for anyone for that matter. I was a young, single mother of two, extremely insecure, and Todd knew it. Sadly, he used this information to his advantage.

Needless to say, Todd and I lived together for just two short months. Our relationship wasn't the healthiest—it was just tolerable. I was extremely insecure, and he had no intention of getting married. The worst part? His constant cheating.

His cheating on me, his lying and deceit, showed his lack of commitment, and I began to realize that my children and I deserved better. When Todd gave me an ultimatum—"You gotta find a career path now or I'll leave!"—in that exact moment I started to wonder if I would now have to "settle," to harshly sacrifice in the important area of love my entire life.

Todd actually seemed embarrassed by my existence. The more and more he disrespected or belittled me, the more and more I missed Isaac. And I found myself reeling backward into depression. In those dark moments, my mind flooded with memories of Isaac treating me like a queen. *"But now look at me! Was Isaac my one and only true love?"*

I thought being with a man would help fill the void in my heart, but in all reality, it made the void more evident. What was I doing wrong? After my break-up with Todd, I found myself lying in bed alone yet again, the room spinning, and all I could do was lie there in an emotional tussle: *"What does my life really mean? What's my purpose for living? I have to keep fighting, keep pushing forward, but how can I? Nothing is working, my pain is so present, but I have to get better for Jordan and Haniyyah."*

I found myself trying to talk to friends and family about my current woes. I was leaning on their words of encouragement to get me through my days of sorrow. Yet, some of their responses and advice left me baffled. It seemed that so many close relatives and friends lacked compassion for me and for my children's emotional well-being.

6 – The Search Continues

I endured their vigorous judgments, though. I recall my friend Dominique saying to me, "Oh, I thought you were over Isaac by now. You had a live-in boyfriend. I thought you were passed Isaac's death."

My ears ached to hear such foolishness. I continued to defend my genuine love for Isaac to so many, yet still no one understood my pain. I tried to explain to them my ongoing grief, but they couldn't relate. They honestly thought that because I had been with Todd, it made my yearning for Isaac disappear, but the funny thing is, I thought the same thing early on. Now, after coming to my senses and breaking it off with Todd, I was becoming angry, shutting myself off from the world.

I wanted so badly for people to understand me, but I was exhausted, trying to convince them of a widow's agony; they weren't hearing me, though, and nothing they could do or say could make my pain go away. I stopped making phone calls to my family and friends to help in the worst times—such as after I had woken up in the early morning with unspeakable pain or after breaking down in the grocery store, leaning on my cart to keep myself from falling.

I continued to dream about Isaac, with dreams so realistic that I wanted to stay asleep just to be with him. I was in this fight alone. Certainly, it was a beautiful blessing to witness my children growing up quickly; however, with each year that passed, with every birthday Jordan and Haniyyah celebrated, I was reminded of their father's death and his absence.

Jordan and Haniyyah had many questions for me over the years. "Mommy, what happened to our daddy? Why did our father have to die? Who shot him? What was he like?"

They were getting older and wiser, and I was so grateful to Rosalyn; she was able to help answer these questions. Rosalyn showed them old photos of Isaac, describing her son to her grandchildren to a T, while fighting back her tears. One of the hardest things I had to witness was my children not only wishing their father were alive but now passionately desiring a father figure. As a parent, you want nothing more than to console your children's hurt, to give them their hearts' desires, but this one thing I couldn't fix. I couldn't bring their father back.

So, I launched myself on a mission for love, trying to locate myself a husband and them an outstanding stepfather, but this mission came to a halt. After my breakup with Todd, I tried dating again, but my relationships were all ending the same exact way: after I would meet a special guy (or who I thought was special at the time) and explain what meant the most to me, what kept me living—meaning my children—that gentleman would show his appreciation by giving me enormous let-downs, disappointments, and continuous deceit.

I felt so bad for my children, but there was a positive aspect: I was waking up out of this nightmare, figuring out there had to be a greater path to unconditional love and happiness. I knew I was causing myself to experience emotional daggers, but was I causing the same for my children? I knew change had to happen. They had been through so much, and now they didn't deserve the disappointments of my relationships as well. I was compelled to do better.

I always appreciated my mom and dad, and tried to instill a great love for them in my kids. My dad helpfully stepped up, offering them a father-figure they didn't have. With my children absolutely adoring my father, we spent a lot of time at my parents' house, and my kids were blessed to feel a fraction of what it was like to enjoy a father's unwavering love.

During the months and years after walking away from Todd, the answer to my despair was finally able to penetrate my heart. One day, I fell to my face in prayer because I was feeling overwhelmed with anger, sadness, and confusion. It all suddenly hit me. I finally came to terms with understanding that my life as I

6 – The Search Continues

knew it with Isaac was so over—and I was at a point of no return. My heart was being held hostage with yearning for Isaac, and I had to break free. Many years had passed me by with my heart stuck in the past—my life stuck in what I remembered love to be.

Yet, there was no going back; Isaac was gone forever. I was experiencing a spiritual shift within me as I remained kneeled down on the floor. Something in me was changing. There was unforeseen comfort, an unexplainable peace. I began to play back the last eight years of my life: I had attempted grief therapy; I had long-lasting companionships; I had a close-knit, loving family; I had two happy, healthy children; I even managed to receive my real estate broker's license after so many people discouraged me, saying, "Stacy, I don't think you're capable of passing the state exam."

I was beating all the odds against my circumstances. Yet, there was a void, a missing piece. Even when Isaac was alive, my soul still didn't feel completely whole. It dawned on me while in this intimate moment with God that the love I had been searching for all these years since the young age of 12 was right there the whole time.

What an ah-ha moment this was! Everything became so clear to me. All this time, my life appeared to have been looking up, from the outside looking in. I had put on a brave face all these years, but my faith was constantly being tested, my soul broken in two. I was hiding in my darkness, but I was beginning to see the light. God didn't allow me to die along with Isaac, even when I begged Him to allow me to. God had kept me. He had a purpose for my life. And this is when it all happened. This is when I came face-to-face with the truth, a stunning turning point—one that brought color and vibrancy to my long-darkened world.

Ask, and it shall be given you; seek, and ye shall find; knock, and it shall be opened unto you.

– Matthew 7:7

7 - TRUE LOVE REVEALED ITSELF

―――――∝―――――

I TRULY CAN'T BELIEVE WHAT I'M WITNESSING … my heart is experiencing something like never before. Is this what unconditional love feels like? I'm stunned in amazement. I thought true happiness was no longer in reach, but now, are my heart's desires finally being fulfilled? Are my weeping prayers finally being answered? Will I finally leave my dark past in my rearview mirror?

Change was really happening. My years of anxiety were finally being lifted.

After Isaac's death, my anxiety has worsened; in those months that turned into years, I was constantly worrying about Jordan and Haniyyah's well-being. My children were getting frustrated, and I really can't blame them. They wanted to hang out with friends and experience the carefree days of being a normal child.

They would sometimes say, "Mom, it's not fair … why can't we go down the street and play with our friends?"

Or, "Mom, why can't we ever have fun?"

I never replied though. I was too ashamed to tell them my truth.

The truth was that I loved them so very much, and I wanted to protect them. I wanted to be where they were to keep them safe. I couldn't bear the pain of harm coming their way. And I always waited for bad news to strike. In the past, death had reached my front doorstep; death had reached my bedside. I feared the life-altering pains of grief.

I was a good person, and still, that horrific chain of events had happened to me. I was overwrought, haunted by my fears ... but now I was beginning to feel a loving peace. I was now experiencing an epiphany, realizing that I was not in control of my tomorrow. Each day I prayed, and the more I read my Bible, the better I would feel. Was this battle finally over?

I was exhaling, I was releasing, I was finally being freed from anxiety. *Is this what it feels like to not be overwhelmed with worry or fear? What a relief!*

So, I came across this Scripture: *"And the peace of God, which surpasses all understanding, will guard your hearts and your minds in Jesus Christ" (Philippians 4:7)*—a verse I would hear my father sometimes quote, and one I was drawn to often. Was I, in fact, able to finally live by it?

I started to look forward to a new tomorrow. I was no longer dreading my future, and I was starting to look at the glass half-full, no longer half-empty. I had a different walk, I had a different talk, my chin was held high, and I was feeling encouraged and inspired. I wanted to live; I wanted to experience what this life here on earth had to offer. There was a newness inside me that brought on a humble confidence—a spark was ignited, and my insecurities were slowly fading away.

For the first time in a long time, my heart wasn't being controlled anymore by trying to date someone, anyone, with hopes to fill an aching void; a void was already being filled—and my heart's desires were being met without any of my doing. My career aspirations were blossoming, and I continued to get visions of business ventures. I thought those visions were odd for someone like me; previously, in my memories that had defined my soul, I had my heart set on only being Isaac's wife, living through Isaac's dream—but now I had my own dreams.

Yet this beautiful, unpredictable moment was suddenly shattered by horrifying news. I received a call from my mother.

7 – *True Love Revealed Itself*

"Stacy, I have something to tell you!" she says.

"What, mom, what?" I answer, my words shaking.

Frantically, anxiously, she continues to talk in almost a whisper ... "Your father has been diagnosed with cancer, but please don't worry; he will beat it."

Just when I thought things were finally looking up, tragedy struck my family again. Anyone who knows me knew I was a daddy's girl. So, I was sitting there, day after day, in a state of shock, yet so hopeful my dad would pull through. I prayed endlessly and tirelessly. There was no way I could bury Isaac, then turn around and bury my father.

My father was such a joy to be around, always bringing laughter to so many. He was my biggest cheerleader. Through all my grief, he was there with me, giving me a shoulder to cry on. He was the only father my children knew. He had to pull through!

"We will beat this!" I encouraged my father, using the same words that I spoke to myself, trying to encourage my anxious heart. "God *will* heal my daddy," I confidently anticipated.

I replayed memories in my head of my father and I dancing in my parents' living room: that was our love language, and oh, how we both loved to dance. I never wanted the dancing to end.

Every childhood memory creeped into my head ... and continued to do so as I stared at the huge, enlarged photo of my father at his funeral. Although I was in disbelief that I was actually preparing to say goodbye to my father forever, I also felt stronger than ever before. The grief I felt with Isaac's death felt different than the grief at my father's. I was beginning to wonder if Isaac's death had prepared me for my father's passing.

Was my new relationship with God giving me this unforeseen strength I didn't think existed? My heart was at perfect peace knowing my father was no longer suffering and with our Lord and Savior. My love for my father was very present, yet my eyes had hated to see him in such agony. Throughout the time both before and after his passing, I found myself giving my mother and siblings words of encouragement; I couldn't believe that I was capable to be in such a role in my own despair. Each day after my father's death, my grief got easier and more bearable, my prayer life got stronger, and I felt I was discovering the cure to all of life's pains.

An old friend even reappeared from my past—someone I had dated for a brief time. Carl reached out to send his condolences after learning of my father's death. He seemed to be extremely compassionate toward my grieving process, and as we began to catch up, I found our conversation highly intriguing. To my great surprise, I even wanted to get to know more about him.

So, when he asked me out for lunch, I replied "yes" without hesitation. And right at that moment, my mind flashed back to a few months prior, when I had given up on love altogether. I had decided I was so over dating and even resolved to become celibate. My annoyance with life then had led me to ask God to take over my love life. I was epically failing in love, and in that split second, I knew for a fact that I wanted God to choose my next husband for me.

So now I started to ask myself questions silently ... *could Carl be the man God has chosen for me? Is Carl the husband my soul is completely deserving of? Is he the husband I've been praying for?*

Because Carl and I managed to hit it off right away, I actually entertained giving dating another shot. I was healing from Isaac's death, and I felt like I was given a brand-new heart. Even though I didn't feel instant butterflies with Carl in our frequent interactions, I really did like him, and I looked forward to eventually feeling those little flutters in my heart once more, the ones I remembered sharing with Isaac.

7 – True Love Revealed Itself

That's where I struggled early on while dating Carl. He seemed to be the perfect guy for me, but I continued to make comparisons with Isaac. It bothered me that we didn't have an immediate connection, so I decided to take a break from Carl to do some more soul-searching. I wanted to be 100% sure that Carl was the one for me. I was very interested in being his friend, I enjoyed his company and his conversation, but I wasn't ready for anything too serious.

Carl, on the other hand, didn't agree to my terms; he only desired to have more. He wanted to be my boyfriend, so I decided to walk away.

I used our time apart to continuously lean on God, asking for more clarity and understanding to untangle my confusion. As I honestly wanted to experience the feeling of being in love again, I committed myself to waiting on God to open up my heart completely. I wanted to be whole, completely healed for whomever God had in store for me, so I remained patient, not caring how long it would take.

Yet after some time apart, I began to miss Carl. I began to wonder, *"What's he up to? Is he dating anyone? Has he had found love and I'm too late? Did I make the right decision by walking away?"*

It was an abnormal emotion for me to over think about my past relationships. I usually walked away from my ex-boyfriends and never looked back. A part of me appreciated that side of me, but on the flip side, it scared me; it scared me that I was able to walk away with so much grace and quickly forgive, even able to maintain friendships with them. I began asking myself, *"Am I unable to attach my heart to someone else's? Is it because I had to bury Isaac (my husband, my first love, my best friend)?"*

So having little patience for any boyfriend who mistreated or disrespected me, I found it simple to deal with little breakups. My heart had been shattered enough, and at the first sign of trouble, I would run away.

But this time was different, I suppose; Carl hadn't done anything wrong, and he had to be special if he was still on my mind. So, one day I decided to call him up, but he didn't answer. I felt strongly that he was ignoring me, and maybe it was too late for us to pick up where we'd left off. Later on that day, however, Carl called me back, and I was so elated. I really did miss him.

He was a little taken back at first ... I could tell in his tone of voice. There was definitely some initial awkwardness in the beginning of our conversation. He started to ask questions about my well-being but seemed more concerned with my dating life.

"Do you have a boyfriend?" he asked.

"No, I really don't."

"Have you been dating though?"

I was a bit bothered by his invasive questioning, but eventually I said, "I have male friends but nothing serious. I've been more focused on getting myself together in our time apart."

Still, I could tell he wasn't too pleased with my reply. I didn't overthink it though, his questioning me. I thought it was just a part of who he was; after all, he was in law enforcement, so he was naturally inquisitive and protective, I thought.

Overall, I was happy about his concern for me, and he obviously still liked me very much. Carl was also still single. And after we talked for some time, that's when we both discovered we missed each other and wanted to give our relationship another try. This time around, I felt I was ready and willing to try love again. I'd had enough time to sort out my feelings, and I didn't want to risk losing a good guy.

The first couple months of dating, I shared everything with Carl. I shared with him my years of hurt from Isaac's death, and I even told him about Jordan's biological father. I was an open book. He appeared to be nurturing toward my heart, and he wanted to be the man he knew I deserved and the stepfather my children needed. He displayed so much character, showing deep concern for Jordan

7 – True Love Revealed Itself

and Haniyyah and continuously confessing his love for me ... then even uttering the word MARRIAGE! Actually, the topic of marriage came up quite often, and I wasn't opposed; Carl was a protector, he wanted to solve all my problems, and he just wanted to love my children and me. As the last ten years of dreadful dating were such a gloomy blur, I was open to receive his love. All I ever wanted was for someone to receive all this love I so badly wanted to give.

Carl's actions allowed me to trust a man again, his behavior made me believe in loving a man again, so after six months of dating, I went with my heart, and I said, "YES!" It was such a memorable moment: he took me to an extravagant restaurant, and out of nowhere, he was down on one knee in front of everyone. I was full of emotions: nervous, bashful, confused, but mostly excited about becoming a wife again. Although those butterflies I wanted so desperately to feel weren't yet fluttering, I started to accept that maybe widows can't have more than one true love. I started to accept that my heart has expanded as much as it could go. Maybe this was life as I knew it for now, and maybe in time I would be head over heels in love with Carl.

I prayed and prayed for this feeling to happen sooner than later, but in the meantime, I would be the best wife I knew I could be. I would give Carl all the love I had to give, I would be loyal and committed, and I promised to never leave his side.

It took five months to plan our wedding, and then it was time to take another trip down the aisle. Locking arms with my brother for that short, momentous walk, I can only say it felt surreal. I wished my father were still alive; I wished he was there to give me away like before. As I stood face to face with Carl, I was in disbelief that I was about to become a wife again. I was overjoyed, knowing God had given me a second chance at marriage. We said our vows surrounded by all of our friends and family, and then as Carl and I walked back up the aisle to exit, to my surprise I noticed some sneers on the faces of some family and friends as well as many empty seats, and I lowered my head with disappointment. I couldn't understand why so many were still not supportive of my happiness and how far I had come.

Did I not deserve to be happy like everyone else? They all knew my past, yet they still frowned upon me. As Carl and I proceeded into the wedding reception, I said to myself, "Today is my special day," and I decided to hold my chin high and enjoy the moment God had gifted to me. As we danced the night away, Carl looked so happy every single time we locked eyes. And although we had married very quickly, I knew who Carl was, I knew he was the right guy for me, I knew he would treat my children as his own.

Carl and I shared the same Christian beliefs, and we even went to marriage counseling, taking all the proper steps to have a successful, lifelong marriage. Knowing I was given a fresh start, I couldn't wait to start our new life together. And I knew things will be different this time around. Yes, losing someone very special to me and seeing my first marriage end so abruptly was out of my control, but now there was no way my second marriage would also end up in disaster.

In that first year as newlyweds, I couldn't believe how fast things were moving along. Carl and I had bought a brand-new home, I opened a brand-new business, and I became pregnant with our baby girl. All my dreams were coming true, and our untraditional family was blending perfectly ... but after giving birth to our daughter KJ, I started to notice some subtle changes in Carl. It started when he stopped sharing a bed with me. He claimed we would only sleep apart for a short time as he didn't want to wake our newborn baby with his loud snoring. Although this decision was concerning, I was initially supportive. Yet I soon began to worry as this space caused a major disconnect between us.

This worry allowed me to embark on a deeper journey in trusting God. I began to pray daily about every single thing that concerned me. My prayer room became my safe haven, and I felt so much peace in God's presence. I would spend many mornings giving God praises and bellowing out cries to Him. The more I stayed in God's presence, the more my heart was healing and becoming capable of being fully in love again, but something was creating a blockade between Carl and me. I so desperately wanted to feel a special connection with my husband, I so desperately wanted to give him every ounce of my heart, but at certain times in our marriage, he seemed to not want my love; it seemed as if he were pushing me away.

I know it sounds crazy, but the moment God began to expand my heart was the exact same moment my marriage took a turn for the worse. The first three years of our marriage was marked by Carl's unpredictable behavior: he never returned to our bed, we lacked intimacy, we continued to argue over the most trivial of topics, and we were drifting further and further apart. Carl and I were beginning to just co-exist, and I could never seem to please him.

"What have I done?" I lamented. "Did I just set my children and myself up for a tremendous let down ... *again*?"

We appeared to be this ideal family, but no one knew I was suffering in a broken marriage. I was hiding the internal bruises from my loved ones, trying to protect my husband's image from the world. Some days would be just like we first met, and then other days we would be like strangers.

Then one day, it happened: the one thing I was trying to avoid all these years. Carl started off by complaining about my role as his wife ... he said I wasn't meeting his expectations ... then he asked me for a divorce!

I couldn't believe what I was hearing. How did we get here? I thought I was doing all the right things, but it still wasn't good enough for Carl. I have always desired to be a loving wife and mother. "We can't get a divorce," I said silently. "This marriage has to work ... I can't fail again with love; I can't fail again with marriage."

I pleaded with Carl, asking, "What can I do to make this marriage work?" He never gave me a direct answer, though, as he danced around the question. He never took any accountability for his mistreatment of me, and we weren't making any headway. The next week after he uttered the word "divorce," things seemed to get back to our normal. He apologized for jumping the gun, and then he expressed his love for me.

"Now this was the Carl I married," I thought. "Maybe it was the stress from his demanding job causing him to act this way?" I hoped that maybe my prayers were being answered, hopeful our marriage would be saved. But after a month or so, Carl said that frightening word again: "divorce!" and then again and again. I was beginning to become numb to this behavior until Carl stopped speaking to me for weeks at a time. I noticed that if I didn't agree with Carl or let him have his way, his absence would be my punishment. I was living in a controlled environment, unable to be my full self. Some days I would just stifle my opinions to avoid him giving me the silent treatment. I was on an emotional rollercoaster, one minute preparing to hire a divorce attorney and the next, planning our annual family vacation. This tumultuous behavior was trying to wear me down emotionally and mentally, but I couldn't let it break me. God had brought me too far, and I refused to go back to a dim depression.

The only solution was constant prayer, but the more I asked God to change Carl and fix my marriage, the worst Carl became. His words became harsher, his presence lessoned, and he completely checked out of our marriage. "Is there someone else?" I thought. "Who did I marry?"

Carl was supposed to nurture my newly beating heart, not try to break it into pieces. *"How can he treat me this way? He knows what the children and I have been through! How could he!? Will I be a single mother again?"*

He was supposed to be my best friend. We were presumed to be one in the eyes of God, but he felt like my enemy. I couldn't allow KJ to grow up without her father in the home like Jordan and Haniyyah. I wanted something different for her. I've always wanted my children to have what I had growing up: a loving, two-parent home. So, I figured I would stick it out. Isaac was taken from me, so I couldn't just walk away. I valued my marriage and what marriage meant to God—so I had to fight for it.

After years of heartache, Carl finally agreed to go to marriage counseling. This seemed like a great antidote for our crumbling marriage, but when we sat before the therapist, Carl wasn't truthful and never accepted any responsibility. Sadly, counseling felt like a big waste of time, and I no longer wanted to attend. I was giving up.

That's when I finally wrapped my mind around getting a divorce and being a single mother once more. And then I mustered up the courage to tell Carl.

"Carl," I said, "I've tried everything to fix our marriage, and I can't go on like this. I don't deserve to be unhappy, nor do the children. I'm ready to proceed with the divorce." Later, I realized I didn't really mean what I was saying at the time, but I felt my back was up against the wall. I was hoping Carl would intervene, claim me as his lifelong partner, and change his ways. And so I was relieved when Carl did just that: he no longer wanted a divorce and said he was willing to try and salvage our marriage. I couldn't believe the miracle! God was changing Carl. He even agreed to attend church with me on Sundays, and we even prayed together. We were on a path of restoration for about six weeks ... until I received an early morning text.

The sound of this text sickened my stomach. I remembered that, in the past, Carl would send me long text messages, expressing his disappointments in me as a wife. I had dreaded to read each and every word. And now I was so scared to see what this text would reveal; I didn't know if I could handle reading any more of his judgements and ongoing complaints. The text read, "*Stacy, we are no longer compatible. I have tried, but this marriage isn't going to work.*" He continued, saying, "*I didn't sign up for this type of a marriage. You have changed, you're not the Stacy I married.*" I was heartbroken again, with another major blow to my soul. But all hope wasn't gone.

Carl was right—there was something very different about me: a newfound strength, a newfound happiness, a newfound joy. I had found comfort in the midst of a storm! The destruction of this marriage didn't destroy me; it actually refined me. Even after all the pains and trauma I had endured over my life, I was actually the happiest I'd ever been. How was this even possible? Carl didn't understand this new me and didn't like the new direction I was taking. Tears rolled down my face as I read Carl's text because I knew in an instant we were over. Something finally clicked: Carl wasn't going to change. And feeling a spiritual release, I heard God say, "*You have endured enough my child, you can now leave this marriage in peace. Carl can only change when he seeks Me for himself, just as you have. You can't change Carl ... only I can!*"

True Love revealed itself to me this day ... and I realized that God had been speaking to me since the day I was born. God was always with me, and He released me years ago from this marriage, but I ignored every feeling or sign out of fear. I finally sat still long enough this time to listen and obey God's Word. Oh, how I cried tears of joy when I heard this while in prayer!

After six years, my marriage came to an end, and God released me. I had fully forgiven Carl and now had no more worries, doubts, or concerns about my marriage. God had given me a supernatural peace.

I also realized how I had evolved spiritually over the course of my marriage. My ongoing pains had drawn me closer and closer to God. It appeared to many that I had found a new love and relationship in Carl, but in retrospect, I found my true love and an even greater relationship in God. Through my marital hurdles, I consistently experienced spiritual encounters with God: I starting to encourage others with God's Word and share with them my ongoing testimony. I was no longer the "old Stacy." In essence, I realized "my why"—my reason for living ... I was walking into my purpose.

I am sure that nothing can separate us from God's love—not life or death, not angels or spirits, not the present or the future, and not powers above or powers below. Nothing in all creation can separate us from God's love for us in Christ Jesus our Lord!

– Romans 8:38-39

8 – MY PURPOSE

MY LIFE HAS BECOME SO CLEAR TO ME—MY "why." The reason why I walk this earth. For so long—from the young age of 12—I was on a quest for love. I had love on my brain but struggled with the feeling of being in love in my heart. I was looking for someone to take my pain away, someone to comfort my aching soul. I was looking for someone to hold me through my lonely nights, someone to give me answers to so many unanswered questions. I didn't know how to handle life's obstacles or balance depression mixed with distrust and disappointment at others' deceit. Then one day I woke up, and my life was never the same—from the moment I discovered God for myself, I discovered my purpose for living and my walk in God.

When I was a little girl singing in the church choir, I felt God's gentle touch every time I would belt out praises to Him through song. I really didn't understand exactly all I was feeling, but in those moments, I know I felt peace, I felt safe, and I felt an indescribable Love. When my innocence was taken away from me at 12 years old, I felt abandoned and alone. I began to soak in my shame and embarrassment. At that young age, I was introduced to the ugliness this world has to offer, and I didn't know how to combat it. Trying to fight a towering battle alone, I entered into unfamiliar territory.

I continued on this same troubling path for a number of years, leaning on my own understanding. As I desperately tried to please and receive approval from others, my insecurities led me to believe the opinions of man—but eventually, this darkened road led me right into the light. Finally basking in this light, I discovered who I was called to be in God, and that all the pain I suffered was for my good. It was for this very moment right here—to help someone else through my stories and testimonies.

Trust in the Lord with all your heart and lean not on your own understanding; in all your ways submit to him and he will make your paths straight.

– Proverbs 3: 5-6

Once I sought God through prayer and reading His Word consistently, a veil was lifted from my eyes. When I surrendered my all to God, I began to feel His heavenly presence immediately. My heart became whole again, better than ever before. God showed me how to fully forgive and love my enemies by allowing my heart to do the unimaginable. I was able to forgive Isaac's shooter, my rapist, Josh (Jordan's biological father), my ex-husband (Carl) … the list goes on and on. I was able to have compassion for those who caused me harm, which gave me the ability to pray for them (my enemies). I never thought I would be capable of forgiving people who had traumatically impacted my life, but the moment I was able to fully forgive was the moment I could be forgiven.

There's healing in forgiveness. In the midst of God's forgiveness and experiencing my own new heart of forgiveness, my heart was changing, my anxiety was lifted, and I was at perfect peace. God was answering my prayers supernaturally and blessing my heart's desire. He promised to carry every single burden if I had faith, so there was no need for me to fret or worry anymore.

And I finally grasped it. I no longer spent my time or energy on things I couldn't control; I was committed to spending my time getting into a stronger relationship with God. And when I did that, an overflow of blessings would follow. What a glorious life! My heart was comforted with unwavering love, peace, and joy … is this what it means to experience heaven on earth? I witnessed many miracles, signs, and wonders of God. I never went back to that old Stacy again; for the first time in my life, I was living.

> *For if you forgive other people when they sin against you, your heavenly Father will also forgive you. But if you do not forgive others their sins, your Father will not forgive your sins.*
>
> *– Matthew 6:14*

> *Cast thy burden upon the LORD, and he shall sustain thee: he shall never suffer the righteous to be moved.*
>
> *– Psalm 55:22*

On my heart-wrenching quest for love, my soul was actually in search of God. I needed only Him, not a man or the things of this world; only He was capable of filling the aching void in my soul. Only His touch could seal the hole in my heart. So, during the times I was married, in a relationship, or receiving gratification through my worldly desires, I still felt a deep emptiness; I still felt incomplete—because God wasn't present in my life.

I wasn't leaning on God, yet He was my only cure. I was looking for love in all the wrong places when Love was starring me right in the face the entire time. All I had to do was call on God; all I needed to do was stretch out my hand to my Lord and Savior, Jesus Christ.

The death of Isaac actually pushed me into the arms of God—as the pain I endured, no human could fix. In my marriage to Isaac, I leaned on Isaac for my happiness and peace, so when he died, I was useless. In truth, Isaac's death really saved my life. The pain of his tragic loss dropped me to my knees as I wept to God to carry my pain.

In other words, Isaac's death launched me on my faithful journey to God. The failures of my second marriage and other relationships pushed me to renew my search for happiness, which allowed me to seek God still more. God promised to comfort my grief, to never forsake me, to fight every one of my battles.

So why was I attempting to do it all alone? God loved me so much that He gave His only begotten Son to die for my sins; I didn't have to fight my fleshly desires, my grief, depression, or attacks alone. This was my wakeup call. This was me surrendering to God, and that's when God opened up the gates of heaven ... .

> *Surrender your heart to God, turn to him in prayer, and give up your sins—even those you do in secret.*
>
> *– Job 11:13-14*

> *Be strong and courageous. Do not be afraid or terrified because of them, for the LORD your God goes with you; he will never leave you nor forsake you.*
>
> *– Deuteronomy 31:6*

8 – My Purpose

For just as we share abundantly in the sufferings of Christ, so also our comfort abounds through Christ.

– 2 Corinthians 1:5

The righteous cry out, and the LORD hears them; he delivers them from all their troubles.

– Psalm 34:17

God did not keep back his own Son, but he gave him for us. If God did this, won't he freely give us everything else?

– Romans 8:32

As I reflect on my life today, I'm so humbly grateful to share how far God has brought my family and me—the young girl everyone whispered about, the teenager everyone counted out, the young lady who thought her life was worthless. That broken woman has grown into a strong woman of God. When I walked into the light, when God redirected my crooked path, my new walk led me straight into my purpose in God.

At the age of 35, I was humbly shocked when God led me to discover a new talent that has blessed me incredibly: the gift of writing. One day, I picked up my computer and started to type, and the words poured onto the paper. I was shocked by what my written words expressed as I trusted God to use this newfound, creative gift. Once I sat myself still in God and gave Him more of my time, I was able to discover my talents, my spiritual gifts, and my purpose. God also gave me many extraordinary visions that led me into the television industry as a content developer, and for several years now, these visions have allowed me to shine as an entrepreneur.

I'm also so grateful to God for allowing me to be an example of His love for my children. Jordan and Haniyyah are doing amazing; they are both excelling as young adults. KJ has always been a vibrant, cheerful child, and she has handled the split between Carl and me extremely well. The hearts of all three of my children are full of love and forgiveness. In addition, my mother and siblings are closer than ever before. The death of my father brought us even closer together, and I'm so blessed to have such a loving, close-knit family. Rosalyn and I have remained very close over the years; she's like a second mom to me. She's very present in her grandchildren's lives and even took on the title of Grandma for little KJ as well.

I have also been able to feel butterflies again. That has been a total surprise and "icing on the cake," so to speak. I didn't think my heart was capable of being in love after such a tragic loss, but God has blessed me to be in love again. Even after a failed second marriage, God's best for me wasn't to be alone for the rest of my life or just to "settle" in love.

I was in utter shock when I felt my heart flutter and be connected to someone's soul. When I completely turned my focus from having a man to strengthening my relationship in God, that was the moment God blessed me with this unexplainable love. My heart loves at a new level now; it simply had to fully heal before I could recognize true love or express genuine love to another.

Yet, I didn't realize this until new love came into my life unexpectedly. Yes, I knew that God was a miracle worker, but now I've profoundly experienced it in a new way. Do you understand how powerful that is?

After my first husband's death, it was like something in me shattered, like a part of me vanished; I was no longer the same. As I currently write this book, I'm reflecting not only on how far God

8 – My Purpose

has brought me over the years but also on how He has confirmed to me the true meaning of "Love."

As I patiently waited on God when beginning this new relationship, a new journey of faith for us both, I constantly sought God for direction; I did things completely different than ever before. A place in my heart was reignited when God connected our hearts together—a feeling that was initially unrecognizable. What I need my readers to understand is that if he and I were to never speak again, I would still be so grateful that God has allowed me the ability to recognize the feeling of true love through this new relationship.

I'm so blessed to be able to experience something I thought was lost forever: the ability to identify unconditional love again, which exemplifies God's unconditional love for me. God's best for me was never to settle, but instead, to love more abundantly than ever before. And I'm a witness to the power of prayer and obedience; God moved in my life so quickly with this new love that it was breathtaking.

Do you understand that God will never give up on us? God has given me another testimony to share—through this new, loving relationship. How merciful God is! That's why I must share these spiritual encounters throughout my life; I recognize every miraculous blessing God has placed in front of me. Many may miss their blessings because they are so blinded by their pain. Yet to be given the opportunity to truly love again is worth treasuring, and I recognize that it's only through God's favor. He truly answers prayers and blesses your heart's desires if you have faith!

When I began to live in God's purpose for my life, I witnessed so many miracles, signs, and wonders of God. Sometimes when we live without purpose or direction, unsure of what we are supposed to be personally, professionally, and spiritually, it can bring on doubt, confusion, insecurities, and depression. It can allow you to take in the wrong advice and connect yourselves to the wrong spirits. But all becomes incredibly clear once you discover who you are called to be in God ... He will answer your many questions, such as what is your purpose for the Kingdom of God? Or why were you birthed? Or how can He order your steps? Do you trust Him with all your heart? Accepting His unshakeable faith? I've discovered all this as I allowed God to open up closed doors.

God will turn those no's into yes's; He will make a way out of no way. We are all made in the image of God, we all have a mighty purpose, and it's bigger than what our minds can even fathom. We must understand that God is there all the time, He loves us unconditionally, and He is just waiting for us to call on Him. You don't have to fight the battles of life alone. You have a Savior to bless you with peace and comfort in the midst of a storm.

Our tests become our testimonies so we can help someone else, and that's why we must share our every testimony to encourage others. Your testimony is your ministry; this is our purpose! We must glorify God all the time, even in sorrow. We must focus on how to draw God's children to the light: God is the Light, and the Light lives within us, which means we are all vessels and servants of Christ. We must work on loving and forgiving our enemies, just as God has forgiven us.

We must seek God in prayer and give Him our time so He can reveal our kingdom's purpose. God hears your prayers; please sit still long enough to hear His answers, and don't give up! Prayer works! Stand on the Word of God. It's your guidebook through life; it's the truth!

I'm a living testimony, and I will continue on this journey for God. Life will give us many obstacles, but we must continue to seek God through them all. Every test that I have passed, my every accomplishment, my possessions, my spiritual gifts and talents, are all for the Glory of God. Everything that I am, and all that I have, belongs to God.

This was all done for my purpose—for who I was called to be in God. It was all for this book, which is my story that turned into my testimony, which led me into my ministry. *The Purpose!* It's the Grace, Mercy and Favor of our living God!

And they overcame him by the blood of the Lamb, and by the word of their testimony; and they loved not their lives unto the death.

– Revelation 12:11

Make your light shine, so others will see the good you do and will praise your Father in heaven.

– Matthew 5:16

Author's Note

GOD'S WORD IS SO VERY PRECIOUS, AND IT'S been a joy to see the verses He's provided for each season of my life. **Yet the following Scripture has become my life verse: it says it all.** *This is what this entire book is about! All the pain I suffered in my life and all the bad things that were meant to cause me harm, distract me, or take me off of my course was all done for my good! I didn't see it while I was in the thick of it, going through it, but God had a great plan in place for my life ... He ordered my steps!*

> **And we know that all things work together for good to them that love God, to them who are the called according to his purpose.**
>
> **– Roman 8:28**

Please now don't miss the following letter ... it's really the most important message of my life and—as God opens your heart to Him—I pray it is for your life as well.

Loved on Purpose

Beloved Readers,

Thank you for allowing me to share my journey with you. My prayer is that it leads you to salvation and healing. I would be remiss to end this book without offering the best Gift you will ever receive in your life: the gift of salvation. If you don't know Jesus as Lord and Savior and desire to surrender your life to Him, or if you are born again and would like to rededicate your life, repeat this prayer out loud and believe it in your heart, and you will be saved and or restored.

> **Father, I admit that I am a sinner and I ask that you forgive me. I believe that you died for my sins and rose from the dead just for me. I turn from my former life and believe that, inviting You into my heart and my life, I am now born again. I trust and confess that You are my personal Lord and Savior, and from this moment on, I will never be the same. I am a child of God! In Jesus' name, I receive this gift of salvation. Amen!**

If you said this prayer and believed it in your heart, you are now saved ... born again. Old things, the former you, are now in the past, and you are a new creature, free from guilt and shame of your former self. Please find a Bible-based church to learn how to walk with Jesus and to enjoy the abundant life He has planned for you.

www.ingramcontent.com/pod-product-compliance
Ingram Content Group UK Ltd.
Pitfield, Milton Keynes, MK11 3LW, UK
UKHW041954230426
12048UKWH00008B/328